Wine Tasting in San Diego & Beyond

Partake of the Grape in San Diego,
Temecula, Baja, Rancho Cucamonga,
and Los Angeles

Janene Roberts

With over 40 wineries listed

2nd Edition

Additional copies of this book can be ordered
using the form on page 208.

Information in this book was researched and edited.
All rates and information are accurate as of press time,
and may have since changed.
Popcorn Press & Media and Janene Louise Roberts are not responsible for
discrepancies or changes.

Library of Congress Cataloging-in-Publication Data

Roberts, Janene.
    Wine tasting in San Diego & beyond : partake of the grape in San
    Diego, Temecula, Baja, Rancho Cucamonga, and Los Angeles / Janene
    Roberts.-- 2nd ed.
        p. cm.
    ISBN 0-9674351-1-0 (pbk.)
        1. Wine and wine making--California--San Diego Region--Guidebooks.
    2. Wine and wine making--California--San Diego Region--Directories.
    3. Wine tasting--California--San Diego Region. 4. San Diego Region
    (Calif.)--Guidebooks. I. Title.

TP557.R62 2004
641.2'2'0979498--dc22

                                                                2004044303

Published in 2004 by Popcorn Press & Media.
P.O. Box 900039
San Diego, CA 92190-0039

Book design & layout by Ellen Goodwin of Ellen Goodwin Graphics.
Edited by Laurie Gibson of Word Association.
Copyright © 2004 Janene Louise Roberts.

First published in 1999.

ISBN 0-9674351-1-0
Printed in the United States of America

Dedicated to my parents, Ed and Barbara Roberts, who allowed me to be serendipitous as a child, helping to form my creative spirit.

Acknowledgments

A lot has changed in the wine tasting community of Southern California since the first edition of this book. Wineries are opening in unexpected places. More and more people are becoming interested in trying new varieties of wine, and less interested in the snob appeal of it. I am grateful to the many people who have come along to support the new version of *Wine Tasting in San Diego & Beyond,* including the support of my friends and family.

Laurie Gibson, my editor, continues to offer her input, advice, and editing skills and has stuck it out with me throughout the years. Thanks to Ellen Goodwin for the redesign both inside and outside.

Thanks to *San Diego Magazine* online for offering me a regular column on their website (www.sandiegomag.com) about the San Diego wine industry, and also to Mike Duran of Allroadstraveled.com for my regular column there as well.

Thanks to all of the wineries that provided information regarding their establishments.

Never did sun more beautifully steep
In his first splendor, valley, rock or hill;
Ne'er saw I, never felt, a calm so deep!

- William Wordsworth

Disclaimer

This book provides information regarding wine tasting in and around Southern California. The purpose is to provide information that is helpful to the wine enthusiast who lives in or travels to Southern California. It is intended to be a fun guide used for leisure activities. You should read and learn as much as possible and then use the information that is best for your needs. You may also want to read other texts to increase your knowledge. See the "For Further Reading" section.

Wine tasting takes time and patience to learn. For many people, the learning process is very enjoyable.

The contents of *Wine Tasting in San Diego & Beyond* have been edited and proofread to make it as accurate as possible. In addition, this information is accurate up to the printing date, but some information may have since changed. Please use this book as a guide and not as a final source of wine tasting information. While planning your trip you may want to verify the information with the establishment you intend to visit.

Popcorn Press & Media and the author are not liable or responsible for any loss or damage both alleged or caused either directly or indirectly by the contents of this book. It should be understood that the publisher and author do not provide health services or other related services. If these services are required, a professional should be sought. Also, traveling to Mexico can sometimes be risky. Please use your best judgment.

Contents

Introduction

The more I learn about the San Diego area wine country, the more excited I become and the more urgent I feel this information needs to be shared with readers. References are continually being made to the likeness of San Diego and the surrounding area's climate to the Mediterranean and the fact that the area may have a better climate than the Mediterranean for winemaking. The Europeans might be jealous and a bit upset with California and its winemaking in something akin to sibling rivalry. Let's not discredit the Europeans but rather learn something from them. They have been where we're going, and we could glean a lot from their experience.

San Diego and the surrounding areas are not nearly as famous as the Napa or Sonoma valleys in Northern California, but that doesn't mean that our time will not come. Wineries are continually opening, and being on the verge of something grand is an exciting discovery.

My goal with this book is to give readers insight from a consumer's standpoint by visiting each winery and experiencing the wine tasting firsthand. I also want to teach readers about wine so that the process does not seem overwhelming. I focused on wineries that are an easy drive from San Diego. Some wine tasting experiences were better than others, but each winery is unique and enjoyable and I can happily say that I didn't have any bad experiences.

What you should always remember when you are tasting wine is that you are the expert of your own tastes; that's what wine tasting is all about. The more you taste and experience, the more you'll realize what you enjoy and that's what your ultimate goal should be. Get ready to discover this new grape land.

A Trip To France

When I went to France in October 1995, one of my most memorable experiences was in the town of Beaune, where I decided to go wine tasting. The Beaune area is beautiful; the landscape is very green and the soil is a sandy clay color. It looks as though all the buildings were made from the soil. I stopped along a cobblestone road and walked toward a park where school children were skipping in lines on the way to lunch. They made faces at me as I took photos of them.

Down the street, I came upon a wine cave and decided to take a peek inside. Two Frenchmen sat outside the entrance to the cave, which looked like it belonged in a fairy tale. It had an arched opening laced with ivy. I stepped inside and saw a dark tunnel that led me underground. The two Frenchmen shouted to the owner in French that I was going inside. The owner, a burly man, with a dark, curled mustache and a large belly, spoke to me in broken English. I have to admit his English was better than my French. The owner looked at me and asked what I would like. I really just wanted a taste of the wine but unless I bought some wine, which was only being sold by the case, my request would have been a *faux pas*. Instead I asked about his wine and he told me a tale I repeated numerous times to my friends and family.

You see, this Frenchman sold Chablis wine; it was one of his specialties. He talked about how in France, there are good years and bad years for wine and that when an exceptionally good year occurs, the wine is labeled "Chablis." In France, Chablis wine is the premium of the crop. He talked some more about the process of winemaking and I listened intently, wanting to soak in the information. Then he told me, with a look of irony, that in his opinion, some man by the name of Gallo had changed that special premium name by placing the name "Chablis" on inexpensive wine. I laughed to myself.

Thus, it may be that the French are somewhat resentful of California and its wine country. However, there are many people who believe that some California wines are just as good as French wines. Therefore, instead of traipsing halfway across the world to taste good wine, first look in your own backyard. As the French would say, "bon appetit."

There are quite a few countries that label any type of white wine "Chablis" and there are a lot of inexpensive wines being produced with that name. In France, real Chablis is a distinctive wine that is produced in the isolated village of Chablis (about 100 miles south of Paris).

A Trip to Italy

I've been curious about Italy because many winemakers in San Diego compare San Diego and Temecula's climate to Italy's. The search took me to Italy in March of 2002. The rolling hills with their Italian cypress and olive tree landscapes were just as expected, but the actual process of wine tasting proved to be less than expected. Don't get me wrong, even the house wines at Italian restaurants are generally of good quality, but the act of driving through the grapevine-covered hills and stopping at a winery to taste a sample of their product proved difficult.

The sixteenth century era farmhouse inn that I stayed at among the hills was also a winery. Upon arrival, my companion and I were given three bottles of their everyday wine (and later two more bottles of their estate vintage) by our English-speaking proprietor. When asked about tasting wine in the area, the proprietor said we had our own tasting with everything he had given us. This was indeed very generous; of the many niceties we received were fresh croissants one Sunday morning, a free lunch for a small inconvenience, and an English newspaper. But somehow it wasn't quite what we were looking for. We wanted the ambiance of a tasting room with other people enjoying their tastings and discussions regarding the soil, climate, and the distinctions between that region and others in the area. Upon further prompting we were told the wineries keep inconsistent hours of operation and sometimes they aren't open to the public. We also later learned about Italians' long siestas in the middle of the day. Perhaps it was the time of year (March is not their usually busy tourist season), the September 11 crisis, or maybe it's just the Italian way.

Although we drove throughout the Chianti region (an area in Tuscany) searching out "fattorias," the Italian word for wineries, none of the places we drove by welcomed visitors. In the small town of Greve of Chianti, we did find a tasting room that appeared to have the entire Chianti region's wine production. Inside the large, brick-lined room were three round tables with bottles of Chianti Classico wines. We were allowed a taste of each bottle for between .40 and .80 euros. At first we were a little reluctant to try because we were the only customers in the room except for a server who spoke just a little bit of English, but we later warmed up when she brought us crackers and toast with samples of their locally produced sausage. We sampled a large range of what the Chianti Classico area has to offer. Chianti wine is made primarily from the Sangiovese grape and most often has a cherry flavor.

The Chianti Classico area is drier than most of central Italy. The hilly forms and shrubbery are reminiscent of a drive to Julian (the charming, rustic mountain town about 80 miles northeast of San Diego).

When I returned from my trip to Italy, I thought I'd ask the vintners around the Julian area if they were growing any Italian grapes.

"I'm growing Nebbiolo, Muscat Cannelli, and trying to bring in Dolcetto planted two years ago," said Alexander McGeary, owner of Shadow Mountain Vineyards in Warner Springs.

"High in the mountains there is more risk because of frost, lack of soil, birds, and other problems," he said. But according to McGeary, his main driving force is the quality of the wine that these grapes produce. He also says that San Diego's soil and climate are similar to Italy's.

Like McGeary, Dave Wodehouse, president of the San Diego Vintner's Association and president and winemaker of Witch Creek Wineries in Julian and Carlsbad, likes to use Nebbiolo grapes for winemaking. He gets his grapes from Temecula, San Diego, and the Guadalupe Valley in Mexico. He said it seems that there has recently been an increase in consumer demand for the Italian varieties. Other Italian grape varieties he uses include Barbera and Mouverdre.

Perhaps the biggest news yet to support the San Diego winemakers' claims to similarity in climate and soil to Italy is the 2002 planting of the first legally imported Brunello di Montalcino grape vines by the Bridges planned community in Rancho Santa Fe. According to an article on winespectator.com, these vines (named after the Montalcino area in Italy) are a clone of the Sangiovese grape, and are the first of its kind to be planted anywhere in the United States.

It remains to be seen if San Diego can produce wines equal in quality to what it has taken Italy centuries to achieve, but if the San Diego winemakers can pull it off, I'll stay home and drink the wine here at a tasting room with friends and strangers crowded around, and good conversation thrown into the mix.

Season of mists and mellow fruitfulness,
Close bosom-friend of the maturing sun;
Conspiring with him how to load and bless
With fruit the vines that round the hatch-eves run…

- John Keats

Wine Tasting Techniques

Tasting wine can be an overwhelming experience, especially if you're just beginning. But there are really only a few steps to remember. Keep in mind that tasting wine involves your senses: your eyes, nose, and mouth. The label will tell you the wine grape variety and vintage.

Try the following steps next time you're tasting wine. It should take you only a few minutes. Write down your impressions in the "Tasting Notes" section at the back of this book.

1. COLOR

Look at the color of the wine while it's in the glass. It should be clear with no film. But don't worry about sediment in red wines and crystals in white wines. These won't hurt you. Also, look at the hue of the wine. The darker the wine, the stronger the taste. However, as red wines get older the reverse is true. Be leery of red wines that are a true red or have hints of orange. Most likely they're too old. White wines are probably too old if there are hints of brown in them. White wines tend to get darker as they age. A good way to see the hue of the wine is to look at it against a white background. Tilt the glass and use a white cloth or paper to look at the wine near the outer edge of the glass.

2. SMELL

This is an important step because your nose can detect thousands of scents. You should first swirl the wine. This will bring out the wine's bouquet. Now breathe in the wine and linger for just a moment. If you're using the back of this book to record your tasting, make a few notes about what you smell. Most often you will smell pleasant odors such as oak, honey, rose petals, and berries. However, you may also smell unpleasant odors. Sulfur dioxide, a burning match smell, is sometimes found in inexpensive white wines. Also, watch out for wine that has a vinegar smell. If you like what you smell, you'll most likely enjoy the taste. Don't worry about what it's "supposed" to smell like–everyone has different impressions.

3. TASTE

Take a sip of the wine. Some people suggest moving the wine around in the mouth and holding it in the mouth for about ten seconds. This will give you an idea of how the wine tastes and feels. Do what you are comfortable with. As you sip, hold the wine on your tongue to determine if it is sweet, sour, salty, or bitter. Saltiness is difficult to detect; sweetness is probably the easiest. Usually white and rosé wines are the sweetest. A bitter wine will have an astringent taste. That's because it contains tannin, which is found in red wine. Tannin is an antioxidant that slows down the aging cycle of red wine. It is found in grape skins, stalks, and sometimes in oak barrels. If a wine is too bitter, try eating some cheese. This will help to reduce the bitter flavor because the protein in the cheese will mix with the tannin and soften the taste. Try "chewing" the wine as you would chew food. You might find different tastes by doing this. Once you've swallowed the wine, note the lingering taste. This is called the "length."

Try to determine why you like one wine over the other, and while you're tasting, note the differences in expensive versus inexpensive wines. It's a good idea to drink water after each taste to clear your palate.

Interested in taking a class on wine tasting? Try the Balboa Park (San Diego) Food & Wine School. The school is in the House of Hospitality and offers wine classes with titles such as "Forget the Wine Geeks, Wine is for Everyone." Contact the school for more information: (619) 557-9441 or www.balboawinefood.com.

Starting a Wine Tasting Group

One of the best ways to learn about wine is to taste it with a group. Many beginners are often intimidated by wine tasting groups, but being in a group where everyone is a willing learner can really forge a path to understanding. If you currently aren't part of a wine tasting group, this chapter will give you some ideas about forming your own (or helping a friend start one).

The group that I taste wine with starts with eighteen people and eight bottles of wine. Getting enough people to help share the cost allows the group to purchase wine that's more expensive than you'd perhaps buy on your own. However, the size of the group isn't as important as the consistency of its meeting. The group I taste with meets once a month. Find people who show an interest in tasting wine, starting with friends, family, and co-workers. Pretty soon you'll be turning folks away.

Although my group uses a form to score wines, you don't have to be that formal. You'll need to pay attention to the wine characteristics in order to take notes and describe what you're tasting, but you can make the tasting rather loose and just talk about it.

According to an article in the magazine *Wine Country Living* (June 2002), a couple in Napa Valley, including Schramsberg winemaker Hugh Davies, have informal three-vintage Sunday tastings and start with the youngest vintage wines first. Like the group I taste with, the Schramsbergs usually sample eight wines at a time and usually have a theme such as "American Pinot Noir" or "Napa Valley Cabernet."

Here are some quick tips to help you get started:

1. Gather a group of people. Eighteen people can conduct an eight-bottle tasting.

2. Buy pouring spouts for your wine bottles. I bought mine at WineSeller & Brasserie. The spouts pour out accurate amounts of wine to allow for approximately eighteen tastes per standard-sized bottle (750 ml).

3. Figure out where and when to meet.

4. Ask each person to bring the appropriate number of wineglasses, or supply enough glasses yourself.

5. Pick a leader (it will probably end up being you if you're organizing the group).

6. Decide on a topic and determine how much the group members want to spend. The group I taste with chooses topics based on wines from a particular region or a single grape variety.

7. Establish judging criteria. My group uses the U.C. Davis 20-point rating scale. I found wine tasting forms on the website www.grapenut.com that are similar to the forms my group uses. Decide if you want to blind taste or not. The group I taste with conducts blind tastings: each participant chooses his or her top three samples, the wines are then unveiled, and the group finds out which wines got the most points. Sometimes the low-cost wines are the favorites.

I've found that tasting wine is sort of like going to college: the more educated you are, the more you want to learn. But regardless of how you set up your tastings, remember to taste wine regularly with the group, and enjoy yourself! Cheers!

If you're not interested in organizing the wine tasting, try calling 1-800-WineShop. According to their literature, this company will bring you a half-case of wines selected from over 200 boutique vineyards–and they'll also conduct the entire tasting.

Local Blind Wine Tasting

I conducted a blind tasting of San Diego and Temecula wines with my monthly wine tasting group in 2002. I wanted group members to sample varieties that are a little different from your standard Chardonnay and Merlot. Thus, I chose the white variety Viognier and the red variety Nebbiolo. We tasted four of each variety. In my prior research I had discovered that the San Diego and Temecula areas are similar in climate and soil to the Rhône region in France as well as parts of Italy. Nebbiolo is from the Northwest Piedmont area of Italy and Viognier is from the Rhône Valley.

Nebbiolo produces a dry red and also a sweet pink wine. *The Essential Wine Book* by Oz Clarke describes the grape as having memorable tastes, but not necessarily enjoyable ones. According to the author, toughness and tannin are the hallmarks of this grape, and these traits often overshadow the finer points. Some words used to describe the wine produced by Nebbiolo grapes are "tarry," "inky," "smoky," and "spicy."

Viognier is often described as an alternative to Chardonnay and is noted for having tastes of peaches and apricots. Other words used to describe the variety include "pear," "melon," "light butter," "vanilla," and "toast."

I looked for local wines in our area stores such as Cost Plus, Trader Joe's, Keil's, Costco, and Beverages & more. Unfortunately, the supply was limited; most of the stores carried local wines only from Callaway and Thornton. In the instance where I found a local wine, it was most often a Cabernet or Chardonnay. I did find Callaway and Thornton Viogniers at Cost Plus (these were part of the tasting).

Another wine I purchased from a San Diego winery was a Witch Creek Nebbiolo. Although the grapes were grown in Mexico's Guadalupe Valley, the wine is made in San Diego.

This winery is known by local winemakers for its Nebbiolo. The other San Diego winery choice was Shadow Mountain Winery's Viognier. Both wineries shipped the wines to me at a reasonable cost.

The remaining supply came from a visit to wineries in Escondido and Temecula. I wanted to purchase a few wines that were notable and perhaps had won some awards for quality. I found an Orfila Estate

Lotus that has won numerous awards including a gold medal in the 2002 Florida State Fair International Wine and Grape Competition. Although it's non-vintage and not entirely made up of Viognier (Marsannee and Roussanne grapes were mixed in, although the majority of the grapes used are Viognier), the wine is notable for its brilliant light gold color and nose of ripe apricot and honeysuckle.

The remaining five bottles came directly from local wineries–a Thornton Nebbiolo, a Filsinger Nebbiolo, and a Callaway Nebbiolo. The most expensive wines were the notable ones from San Diego: the Orfila Estate Lotus Viognier and the Witch Creek Nebbiolo.

Not surprisingly, the members of my wine tasting group voted a tie for first and second place of the Orfila Estate Lotus and the Witch Creek Nebbiolo. The third choice was the Thornton Viognier purchased at Cost Plus. The label describes the grape-growing area as "South Coast"; most likely this means the grapes came from the coastal appellations of Paso Robles or Santa Barbara. Both Thornton and Callaway seem to be following a trend that Mondavi, BV, Kendall-Jackson, and Beringer started: purchasing grapes from this region in order to sell reduce-priced wines.

The Temecula wines may have suffered in the tasting due to the area having problems with Pierces disease, a vine-choking bacteria that hinders the vines' ability to absorb water, and thus at the time of the tasting, Temecula had lost thousands of acres of vines. San Diego vintners seem to have learned a lesson from Temecula grape growers and have thus far mostly avoided the disease by planting varieties that thrive in the climate, rather than planting grapes in response to market demands.

Because of the Pierces disease problem in Temecula, however, the wineries there have been experimenting with planting other varieties and have updated their growing techniques. Some wineries are planting their vineyards in small blocks instead of the old, large-block format and they're modifying with a diverse mixture of grape varieties.

The wine tasting group's overall consensus was that although the top two wine choices showed promise, they were overpriced. The rumblings in the group seemed to indicate that the perception of local wines is not very good. In order to compensate for this mind-set, local wineries might need to try harder to produce consistently good wines that are competitively priced.

Selecting Wine for a Party

So you've offered to bring a bottle of wine to a dinner or party? Why not choose a local wine to present at the table? You would be supporting the regional wine industry (a growing one at that), which would also make for a nice topic of conversation during dinner.

Although San Diego wines may be a little bit more expensive than mass-produced wines, take the Slow Food approach and invest in preserving San Diego's unique taste. The Slow Food movement was started in 1989 by a man named Carlo Petrini.

Petrini came up with the idea for Slow Food after a McDonald's restaurant opened on the Spanish Steps in Rome. According to the book *Slow Food* (Petrini is the author), Slow Food began as a "gastronomic organization developed to rediscovering and protecting the right to enjoying the pleasures of the table and to using our tastebuds as guides to seeking the highest achievements in taste." It was primarily a wine and food association.

In 1996, the movement shifted its attention from gastronomy to ecology. This put the focus more on the land and farmers who produce fine artisanal foods. Thus, it became important to know where the food came from, who produced it, and how to secure a future for its existence. There are about 5,000 members of the Slow Food movement in the United States. The movement concentrates on holding tastings, educational workshops, and major food events.

Just think how sophisticated you'll seem when you bring up the topic of Slow Food at your next dinner party while enjoying a bottle of good wine from a local vintner.

Thy glass will show thee how thy beauties wear,
Thy dial how thy precious minutes waste;
The vacant leaves thy mind's imprint will bear,
And of this book this learning mayst thou taste.

- William Shakespeare

Benefits of Wine

In May 1990, an article appeared in *HEALTH Magazine* that addressed the "French paradox." Even more people heard about this issue on a *60 Minutes* television segment based on the article. The basis of the paradox was that French people (who consume a lot of cheese, meat, butter, and red wine) have half the death rate from heart disease as that of Americans. The study concluded that people who drink in moderation–two glasses each day–develop heart disease less frequently than people who don't drink at all and people who drink heavily. This new, hopeful information gave people a reason to stock up on their wine supplies. Then medical researchers declared that wine was not only good for you, but all kinds of alcoholic beverages were good for you. They maintained that the alcohol in the drinks kept arteries unclogged because it raised HDL cholesterol levels and kept the blood from clotting. However, in 1995 a Copenhagen heart study found that the effect of beer on mortality rates was minimal and liquor's effect was actually connected to increased heart disease rates. It found that regular wine drinkers had the least instance of heart disease.

Another study, conducted at the University of California at San Diego School of Medicine, determined that the lowest amount of heart disease was found among people in countries that had the highest rate of wine consumption. Researchers also found that the lowest heart disease rates occurred where people ate a great deal of fruit. The idea stems from the presence of phenolic flavonoids found in wine's non-alcoholic compounds (natural antioxidants). Phenolic flavonoids are found in the skin, seeds, and stems of red grapes. Antioxidants are believed to be one factor that protects bodies from oxidation. Oxidation of LDL cholesterol may lead to artery blockage and heart attacks. Thus, phenolics may disrupt this pattern.

Fresh fruits have a high concentration of phenolics and wine, after the fermentation of grapes, has an increased concentration of the chemical. Red wine has an exceptional amount of phenolics because it contains whole-fruit extracts.

However, some people are still skeptical of these findings and note that alcoholic drinks are associated with other health risks. These include esophageal, throat, and mouth cancers, liver disease, and breast cancer. But these risks may be associated with the actual alcohol content of the drinks; some experts say that the phenolic antioxidants of wine counter these problems.

People are drinking wine more frequently in part because it has been proven to raise HDL cholesterol, and thins the blood a little. Supposedly, these factors protect against heart disease.

However, do not think of wine as a cure-all; rather, it should be something to enjoy and used with restraint.

In any event, as the experts research the facts, the best advice is to drink in moderation and remember to drink responsibly and designate a driver for the ride home. So, sit back, relax, and enjoy one to two glasses of wine each day.

Serving Wine

Some people believe that each wine requires its own unique glass. The reason is that the shape of the glass determines how the wine is received on the tongue. It is recommended that red wines, especially those that are young, be drunk out of glasses that have larger bowls with rims that have a slender inward curve to keep the wine from spilling. The larger bowls allow swirling of the wine, which causes aeration. Most people, however, do not have a large collection of glasses. Your best bet is to purchase good all-purpose wineglasses with 10- to 12-ounce bowls.

When you are at a restaurant and ordering a nice-quality wine, make sure the waiter gives you appropriate glasses and fills the glass half full so that there is enough room for swirling. If you order an expensive bottle of wine and the waiter brings out small-bowled glasses, ask if more appropriate glasses are available. Otherwise, you're better off ordering a less expensive bottle since you won't be able to distinguish the variations of aroma and taste with small-bowled glasses.

If you're at a restaurant and a waiter gives you the cork of the wine you ordered, don't sniff it–check for intactness, not scent. However, many corks are now made of plastic instead of cork because the natural ones can leak or fall apart. To stay with tradition, a lot of the higher-priced wines continue to use cork. It remains to be seen if all wine corks will become plastic.

Here are some suggestions for serving wine at home:
- Wash your wineglasses by hand using hot water and a small amount of soap. Then dry the glasses by hand for sparkling stemware.

- Store wineglasses with their bowls facing up so that the rims do not carry the smell of your cupboard.
- Wine can sometimes taste better in thin glasses that have lean rims.
- Youthful wines need large glasses to help tannin emanate.
- Remember to hold the wineglass by the stem. It is possible that the heat from your hand placed on the bowl could affect the wine's temperature.
- Fill the glass no more than half full to allow room for swirling.
- Serve water with wine to allow for cleansing of the palate.
- When serving various bottles of wine, start with a young wine and then move on to an older one. If you are serving whites and reds, start with whites and progress to reds. Other considerations include starting with a light wine and moving on to a more robust one as well as starting with a dry wine and moving on to a sweeter one.
- White wines should be chilled about a half hour before serving. Cold white wines should be taken out of the refrigerator 20 minutes prior to drinking. After the desired temperature is reached, put the white wine in a temperature-controlled wine urn.
- If you would like to chill red wine, chill it for 20 minutes just before drinking it.
- Wine that you have leftover can be stored in the refrigerator with the cork back in but complex wines won't last as long as less complex ones, so generally the more expensive the wine, the better it is to drink it the day it was opened.

Wine History

Wine has been around for thousands of years. However, there is debate over how wine was first created. It has been said that archaeologists found grape seeds and winemaking tools in prehistoric caves and that traces of Egyptian vineyards have been found that go back to 3000 B.C. However, most historical evidence dates to about 1000 B.C. At that time, wine was introduced to Italy and France during the Greek Empire expansion. During the Roman Empire, the Romans mastered the process of aging wines and used barrels and bottles that are similar to the ones used today. As Romans occupied Europe, they brought their wines and vines with them. Some people credit the Romans for laying the groundwork for the famous French vineyards of today, including those in Provence, the Rhône Valley, Bordeaux, Burgundy, and Loire.

In the Middle Ages, the Roman Catholic Church took over the wine trade and monks began using wine for religious ceremonies as well as for recreation. During this time, the church owned a large number of vineyards in Europe. It was then that many of the terms and techniques used in winemaking today were formed.

In early America, Thomas Jefferson enjoyed wine and often went to France to purchase wine for himself and George Washington, James Madison, James Monroe, and John Quincy Adams. When Jefferson was the U.S. Ambassador to France, he explored the wine regions of Europe. In the 1770s he invested in The Wine Company, which produced wine, oil, and silk.

Amazingly, California's most infamous events, earthquakes, are what actually make the state such a prime place for growing grapes. The soil becomes richer as the earth's plates grind together. As different soils are created, they make varied growing conditions. Therefore, the more varieties of soil, the more varieties of wine can be produced through planting different grapes in different soils.

As Southern California continues to grow in population, so does the number of vineyards. However, the population changes through the years have changed the locations of wine regions.

San Diego was the first Southern California area to grow grapes for winemaking. Some people say that it was Franciscan missionary Father Junipero Serra who planted the vines in 1769 at the Mission San Diego de Alcala. Other people debate that assertion. The missionaries traveled from Baja California and established twenty-one missions and planted what was called the mission grape variety for sacramental and medicinal uses. The missionaries were the only viticulturists in California for about 60 years. In the 1820s, the first commercial grower was Joseph Chapman in the Los Angeles area and then in 1831 the Frenchman Jean Louis Vignes brought the first vines from Europe to Southern California. Now, instead of a vineyard, that area has become downtown Los Angeles.

With the Gold Rush came a greater desire for wine and the local winemakers soon had competition from many European winemakers.

In the 1850s a man named Agoston Haraszthy went to Europe and came back with 100,000 vine cuttings, which made a large impact on the number of grape varieties winemakers could use. He brought European varieties to Southern California and later moved to Sonoma, where his vines adapted easily. His contributions were the beginnings of the transformation from the mission grape to the European varieties.

By the end of the 1800s, quite a few Europeans had established wineries in California. The industry was hit with Prohibition two decades later and only a few wineries endured (by manufacturing wines for religious ceremonies or growing grapes for home winemaking use). Many wineries had to start all over again once Prohibition was repealed. These early winery sites no longer exist.

There was a demand for wine after Prohibition but the wines produced in California at that time were inferior to ones produced elsewhere. To maintain the status of California's wine industry, The

Wine Institute was developed in 1934. This institute helped organize quality and labeling guidelines. Today, The Wine Institute is based in San Francisco and serves as a public policy advocacy association for California wineries. From the 1930s until now the wine industry in California has grown and continues to show an expanding market.

In the 1980s the largest winery area near San Diego was the Cucamonga district between Ontario and Fontana in San Bernardino County. Unfortunately, human population also grew in this region and began pushing out the grape-growing areas. Thus, several vineyards opened in Temecula (first called "Rancho California"), which was south of the Cucamonga district, north of Escondido, and only about an hour's drive from the mission in San Diego.

Grape Glut

There have been many wine industry articles that mention that prices for the 2002 vintage will be reduced due to an oversupply of grapes that year. But according to Dave Wodehouse, winemaker at Witch Creek Winery and president of the San Diego Vintner's Association, pricing for San Diego wines most likely will not follow this trend because San Diego has a continual shortage of grapes grown in the area. "Pricing in the bigger producing areas and in Central [California] may be affected, but it's just a huge glut of mediocre grapes, not of a lot of quality grapes," he said.

He said his winery deals with a lot of small grape suppliers on a long-term basis and thus prices don't fluctuate as much for him. He did mention, however, that Temecula has too many Chardonnay grapes and that a number of these grapes were not picked in 2002. Wodehouse said that Temecula wineries, in times of grape shortages, sell grapes to Napa Valley and other areas.

He stressed, more importantly, that normally San Diego has chronic shortages of grapes; supply is therefore the biggest concern for San Diego wineries.

Mike Menghini, owner and winemaker for Menghini Winery, seems to echo Wodehouse's sentiments. He said that he doesn't ask his suppliers for discounts in times of oversupply because he has long-term relationships with them.

"There is a glut of grapes out there. Temecula has 100 tons (of

Chardonnay) on the vines because throughout California, grapes are overplanted."

Menghini plants and harvests Sauvignon Blanc, Pinot Grigio, and Cabernet Sauvignon grapes. He said that in San Diego some vineyards are down by 50 percent in their supply. The 2002 and 2003 were strange growing years for San Diego, according to Menghini, because the plants need rain even when they are irrigated. He said that the plants somehow seem to know that it's a drought year. Menghini said his apples are smaller; he's noticed other crops in the area with the same problem.

The current overabundance of grapes is apparently not affecting the price of San Diego wines because the area is a small grape-producing region (in areas where more grapes are grown, there may be more room for reduced prices).

Shipping Wine

Many people don't know that some states do not allow shipment of wine. One of my clients, who owns a shipping franchise, mentioned that some of his customers don't inform him of what they're sending; his company could then become liable for sending product that is prohibited. So, it's important that you know if you can legally ship that Orfila Syrah you're planning to send to Aunt Martha in Alabama. Unfortunately, sending wine to that state is prohibited. You need to know what the laws are for the state you're sending wine to. In some states shipping wine direct is considered a felony. The following is a list of the legal agreements with regard to wine shipments as of this writing. Laws may change, so check with the state before shipping wine.

Reciprocal Agreements (Reciprocal means that the shipment of wine is allowed if the other state has the same agreement).

California	Missouri
Colorado	New Mexico
Hawaii	Oregon
Idaho	Washington
Illinois	West Virginia
Iowa	Wisconsin
Minnesota	

Restrictions/Special Agreements (Check with the individual state for specific rules.)

Alaska	Nebraska
Arizona	Nevada
Connecticut	New Hampshire
Florida	North Dakota
Georgia	Pennsylvania
Louisiana	Rhode Island
Maryland	Texas
Michigan	Washington, D.C.
Montana	Wyoming

Prohibited

Alabama	New York
Arkansas	North Carolina
Delaware	Ohio
Indiana	Oklahoma
Kansas	South Carolina
Kentucky	South Dakota
Maine	Tennessee
Massachusetts	Utah
Mississippi	Vermont
New Jersey	Virginia

Grape Varieties

Did you know that the names of grape varieties have only appeared on bottles of California wines since the 1950s? Before that time, generic names were given to California wines that contained just one variety. In California, wineries now label their wines by the grapes from which they are made. Single varietals are wines made from one grape. When a wine is labeled "Chardonnay," it must consist of 75 percent of that grape variety. Single varietal wines are regarded as the best. However, they are not always an indication of quality. European wineries have a much more complicated way of labeling their wines. They consider the area in which the grapes are grown. The place of origin is not as important for California wines as it is for those in Europe. Since 1983, American Viticultural Areas (AVA) have begun to be established in California. An AVA is a type of appellation where winegrowers in certain areas will ask the government to grant them the right to put that area's name on their wine labels. If the right is granted, 85 percent of the wine in those bottles must be from that area.

Characteristics of grape varieties depend on local climates and customs, but for the most part, grape varieties are consistent. The two most important categories of California wines are varietal and generic.

Varietal wines contain at least 75 percent of one variety of grape and are named after that grape. Generic wines are a blend of different grapes. You may find that a number of bottles are labeled "Meritage." This means that the wine combines Bordeaux varieties like Cabernet Sauvignon and Merlot.

Another name found on labels is a proprietary name. Wineries may label their wines with this name for marketing purposes. The proprietary name used to be on the label instead of a generic name, but now the proprietary name is being used instead of a varietal name for the winery's best wines.

An article in the *San Diego Union-Tribune* in August 2002 mentioned that French scientists have charted the DNA of wine, and can now determine if the wine in a bottle matches its label. According to the article, this is the result of an increasing number of inexpensive wines being sold for far more than their worth. In France, the French government takes this offense seriously and in some cases will fine and imprison sellers of fraudulent wine.

The following are the most common types of varietals found when wine tasting in and near San Diego:

Aleatico

A red variety most often used to produce a dessert wine. The wines are often described as "sweet."

Barbera

A red variety that grows in Italy and California. It has a high acid level. The wines it produces are dry.

Cabernet Sauvignon

A red grape from Bordeaux, France, it produces a wine that is naturally high in tannin. It is produced into dry, red, white, and pink wines. Some people describe the wine as smelling of black currants, cassis, dried herbs, and bell pepper. Most connoisseurs describe it as having depth because it is more complicated than Merlot. Sometimes Merlot is mixed with this variety to add softness.

Carignane

A red grape from Southern France best grown in warm regions. It produces a dry red wine and is sometimes mixed with Grenache, Syrah, and Cinsault.

Chardonnay

A white grape from Burgundy that is very popular in California. It produces a white wine with moderate acidity, which is often aged in oak barrels; therefore, almost all of these wines have an oak taste. The wine can smell of grass and herbs. It is often described as having earth flavors, hints of melon and fig, and can achieve a high alcohol content. Other words to describe this wine include fruit, vanilla, and butter. It is often mixed with Sémillion.

Charbono

A red grape from Northern Italy. It produces a full-bodied, dry red wine. Only a few wineries grow this variety.

Chenin Blanc

A distinct white grape that was very popular for about 10 years, but its popularity has recently declined. It is grown mainly in California, Washington, and Texas. The Loire Valley in France produces Chenin Blancs that are different from the American versions. The French versions have a sharp, acidic taste and are called Vouvray (named after the district they come from in the Loire Valley). In the United States the taste of Chenin Blanc is primarily dry or semi-dry. These white wines tend to have a fruity taste and are sometimes produced widely and then made into a jug wine or a generic blend.

Cinsault

A large black grape that was formerly called Black Malvoisie. Only small amounts of this grape are grown in California. Most often it is blended with other wines to offset a high alcohol content.

Dolcetto

A red variety, the Dolcetto grape is purple and originally from the Piedmont region in Italy. The wine is meant to be drunk young and can be described as full, dry, and soft with a fruity taste.

French Colombard

A white variety that is planted extensively. It can produce wines that have some acidity and is often made into an inexpensive, dry white wine.

Fumé Blanc

Also known as Sauvignon Blanc.

Gamay/Napa Gamay

A red grape believed to be from Southern France. It produces light-to-medium-bodied wines that are dry and red or pink with a fruity taste. Most of the time they have either little or no oak aging (wine that sits in oak barrels) and are produced by a technique called carbonic maceration. Drink these wines when they are young, within about six months to a year of the vintage. This will keep the freshness of the fruit alive.

Gewürztraminer

A white variety that produces a dessert wine that is dry or medium dry. The grape is grown in cool regions. The wine has a spicy and flowery smell and is often described as "sweet" and "tart." It usually has an intense flavor and is generally low in alcohol. "Gewürz" means "spicy" in German.

Grenache/Grenache Rosé/White Grenache

A red grape variety from Southern France. The California variety produces wines that have hints of strawberry and citrus. The wine is light in color and is sometimes produced as a rosé. Wines the grape produces are usually dry and medium-dry or are pink or red in color.

Merlot

A Bordeaux red variety that has been popular since the 1990s. The wines are sometimes described as having scents of chocolate, plum, and earth. Most people describe Merlot as smooth. Sometimes it is blended with Cabernet Sauvignon to add strength to its character. Merlots mature quicker than Cabernet Sauvignons and can be enjoyed as a younger wine. The wines produced are dry and pink or red and have moderate tannin.

Mourvèdre/Mataro

A red Mediterranean variety that is most often blended with other wines. California wines made from this varietal have an herbal character.

Muscat

Exists as both a red and white variety. The grape has aromatic characteristics that may be fruity, spicy, or floral. The grapes are often used to make dessert wines or Italian Spumante.

Nebbiolo

An Italian variety that produces wines that are dry red and also sweet pink.

Petite Sirah (Syrah)

A dark-skinned red variety, it produces a very dark red wine and sometimes produces a pink wine. The wines usually have a black pepper taste and aroma and can be jammy (a heavy, jam-like taste). The California variety really isn't a variety at all; it usually consists of four or more varieties. The wine has a good deal of tannin and is dry.

Pinot Grigio

A white grape from Italy that makes a white wine with lemon and vanilla flavors.

Pinot Gris

A red variety that is a variation of Pinot Noir. It produces a simple dry white wine.

Pinot Noir/Gamay Beaujolais

A red grape from the Burgundy region that is sometimes described as a grape with "personality" and "sensuality." It produces a red wine that is naturally low in tannin. It tends to be fruity, crispy, and with a light body. The wine can have the taste of spices and berries. Its color is lighter than red wines such as Merlot or Cabernet Sauvignon. For some time it wasn't very successful in California. That may be because it's hard to grow in the area. It thrives in areas that are low in temperature and overcast. The areas best suited for Pinot Noir grapes in California are places like Santa Barbara.

Riesling/Johannisberg Riesling/White Riesling

A white variety that tends to be fruity and floral. The grape has high acidity and thrives in a cool climate; it grows and matures slowly. It is grown in California, but tends to be milder than its cooler-region counterparts. The wine is more popular in Europe than in the United States. Most great Rieslings can be found in Germany, Austria, and Alsace, France.

White Riesling is a wine produced from grapes cultivated in California, while Johannisberg Riesling is named after grapes grown in Germany. The latter produces a dry to medium-dry white wine.

Sangiovese

A red grape from Italy. These wines tend to be a medium-red color and are often described as having hints of cherry or smoky flavors.

Originally from Tuscany, Italy, this variety is becoming very popular in the hotter regions of California, such as the Temecula Valley. Results in Temecula so far have been promising. This grape produces the wine called Chianti. Chianti is meant to be drunk young and is sometimes mixed with other varieties.

Sauvignon Blanc/Fumé Blanc

A white variety that tends to be very acidic. This gives the wine a dry, crisp taste. Sauvignon is derived from the French word "sauvage," which means "savage" or "wild." Some people describe it as a stubborn wine. The wine can be sharp, brisk, and lively. Many American wines are a tamed-down version of the true Sauvignon Blanc because many winemakers feel that the true wine is too bold for Americans. In California some Sauvignon Blancs are called Fumé Blanc. These wines are declining in popularity in favor of Chardonnays. In warm regions, these white wines tend to have hints of spice, citrus, pear, and some earthy characteristics.

Sémillon

A white variety originally from the Bordeaux region in France. The grape produces a dry-to-sweet white wine. The wine has scents of spice and fig. It's often blended with Sauvignon Blanc; this combination is sometimes labeled "Meritage."

Syrah

A red variety from the Rhône Valley, France. Words used to describe the Rhône wines are "leathery," "damp," "robust," "earthy," "smoky," "pepper," and "spicy." The California Syrahs produce spicy dry red wines. This isn't the same variety as Petite Sirah, which produces a darker, tannic wine.

Viognier

A white variety from the Rhône Valley, France. This variety is showing great promise in the Temecula region. Sometimes the wine it produces is described as having tastes of peaches and apricots.

Zinfandel

A red grape that is one of the most widely planted in California. Zinfandel grapes are versatile and produce a dry red wine or rosé wine.

Zinfandels are mostly a California variety because hardly any other wine region in the world grows it. There is debate over where the grape originated, but the consensus is that it is of European origin and of a variety called "vinifera." Cooler regions tend to produce a wine with distinguishable tastes of spice and berries. The grape produces a range of wines from light White Zinfandels to rich Zinfandels. They can be made into white wine or even sweet port.

Zinfandel wine is often confused with White Zinfandel wine. The biggest difference is that Zinfandel wines are red and White Zinfandel wines are pink. Zinfandel wines are often described as big and strong. Some people say that the best way to use a Zinfandel grape is to make a true Zinfandel. "Jammy" and "chewy" are sometimes used to describe this wine, and hints of blackberry, spice, and boysenberry can be detected.

White Zinfandel is a light-pink colored wine. Grapes used to produce this wine are picked earlier and have less color and sugar than the grapes used for red Zinfandel. The color of the wine is created by removing the red skins of the grapes before a deep color can be produced. This wine is often thought of as a young person's wine and is often not taken very seriously. Words used to describe this wine are "sweet" and "weak."

Wineries of San Diego County

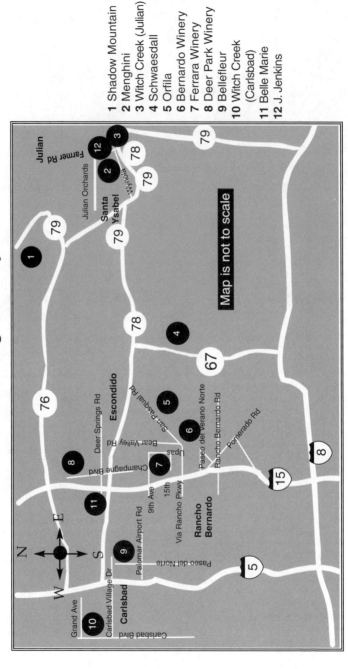

1 Shadow Mountain
2 Menghini
3 Witch Creek (Julian)
4 Schwaesdall
5 Orfila
6 Bernardo Winery
7 Ferrara Winery
8 Deer Park Winery
9 Bellefleur
10 Witch Creek (Carlsbad)
11 Belle Marie
12 J. Jenkins

Map is not to scale

Wineries of San Diego County

San Diego has wineries in various parts of the county. There are three main areas where the wineries are grouped: Rancho Bernardo/Escondido, Carlsbad, and the Julian/Ramona area. You will probably want to make a separate trip to visit each. There is a private winery that sells their wines to local restaurants and markets called **San Pasqual Winery**, but they do not have a tasting room. You can purchase their wines directly from their website, www.sanpasqual-winery.com.

If you're looking for a place to spend the night in San Diego, you might try the **Heritage Park Bed & Breakfast**. The phone number is (619) 234-2926. The address is 2470 Heritage Park Row in Old Town San Diego and the wineries are about a half hour to an hour drive from there. This Victorian house has a two-night minimum on weekends and they serve a full breakfast as well as afternoon tea. You'll also find suites with Jacuzzis.

If you would like to stay at a B & B in another area, try calling the B & B Guild of San Diego at (619) 523-1300.

If you like to taste wine while boating, check out **Cheers**, "The Happiest Boat in San Diego." It holds up to 49 passengers at a time, and offers various wine tasting events throughout the year. Call (619) 200-7417 or visit www.sandiegocharterboatcompany.biz.

Rancho Bernardo/ Escondido

Rancho Bernardo and Escondido are marked with rolling hills between the sea and the desert. The area produces many avocados, citrus fruits, and grapes. It was once a well-respected wine district but lost its distinction after Prohibition. Only now is it regaining its vineyards.

If you would like a nice place to stay in the Rancho Bernardo/ Escondido area, try the **Rancho Bernardo Inn**. The phone number is (858) 675-8500, and the address is 17550 Bernardo Oaks Drive. The inn is well known in the area for its golf course and restaurant. A stay includes a full breakfast at the Veranda Restaurant. The facilities include a golf course, spa, pools, Jacuzzis, and tennis courts.

A lower-cost alternative is the **Holiday Inn** in Rancho Bernardo. The phone number is (858) 485-6530, and the address is 17065 West Bernardo Drive.

Belle Marie Winery

Fog drifted in and out of the Escondido hills as I drove to Belle Marie Winery early one Saturday morning to witness my first grape crush. I remembered watching Lucille Ball stomping grapes in a long-ago TV episode, and expected to see men and women, their pants rolled to their knees, jumping around in large pails of grapes.

Although the scene before me was quite different from that (I realized there would be more machinery and fewer people), I did meet a woman with her sleeves pulled up, wearing plastic gloves, and standing on a plastic pail. She was wearing gloves to work with the cold-stored grapes (50–60 degrees, so the winery doesn't have to use many sulfites to preserve them); she made sure leaves weren't falling into the grape's crushers.

I watched the crushing process. A cluster of purple grapes fell through three rubber wheels into a chute. The wheels crushed open the skins of the grapes, allowing the juice to escape; the grapes were then torn from their stems (the winery sends the stems to a nursery for compost). I witnessed the crushing of the red Spanish grape Tempranillo. This grape is originally from South America, but the winery gets its supply from the Guadalupe Valley in Mexico.

The grape crush is a daylong project. From the grape crusher, the grape juice and skins (red wine only) travel through clear plastic tubes to a stainless steel tank. The red grapes ferment to alcohol for about 8 days and then, once the fermentation is complete, they remain in the stainless steel tanks for 2 to 3 months. The juice is then stored in oak barrels for 1 to 2 years. White grapes remain in the steel tanks for approximately 6 to 8 months, and then are bottled.

I tasted a sample of Zinfandel grape juice, deliciously sweet, and was shown a pail of grapes that were cold-soaking in a large plastic box. (Aha! The image of Lucille Ball's experience was getting more vibrant as it got closer to reality.) Although I didn't get to put my bare feet into the pail with the grapes, I did witness Dan, my host, put his bare fingers into the juice (which was actually a mix of purple grapes skins, juice, and seeds).

This year's crush was 2 to 3 weeks late, he said, because of the humid weather. He pulled out a grape seed from the juicy extract and explained that the seed should be brown (which it was). If the seeds are green, he said, it's better to wait until they brown. According to Dan, this can sometimes be a problem because the sugar content can be right, even though the seeds are still green.

The winery workers then put a hydrometer into the grape juice to measure the sugar content, which is best at 24 to 25 percent. Dan and I walked through the winery while he explained and described the details of the grape-crushing process. As the aroma of grapes, stems, and alcohol all mingled together, I imagined the era when people really celebrated harvest times and rejoiced in the process of making food and drink from scratch. Maybe things haven't changed that much from the days of Lucille Ball's grape crush episode—and in the generations before that (yes, people have been replaced by machinery, but I'm sure this makes the process a lot easier). We can still rejoice in the simple pleasures of savoring the new harvest while enjoying the fruits of our labors.

 LOCATION: 26312 Mesa Rock Road (near the Deer Springs Road exit off I-15 north) Escondido, California 92026 (760) 796-7557

 WEBSITE: www.bellemarie.com

 HOURS: Daily from 11 a.m. to 5 p.m. (winter) 11 a.m. to 6 p.m. (summer)

 TOURS: By appointment.

 TASTING CHARGE: $5.

 WINES AVAILABLE: The winery focuses on "Meritage" wines: wines with a mixture of grape varieties, for example a mix of Cabernet Sauvignon and Nebbiollo.

 DIRECTIONS: Take I-15 toward Escondido and exit at Deer Springs Road, heading west. Make a left at Mesa Rock Road. The winery is on the right.

Bernardo Winery

Bernardo Winery's rustic setting is surrounded by antiques and is right in the middle of a residential area. A number of new, large estate-like homes sit on a hill overlooking the winery. Bernardo Winery is one of the oldest regularly operating wineries in Southern California. It was established in 1889 and then was bought by the Rizzo family in 1928. Ross Rizzo took over in 1962 from his father, Vincent Rizzo, and currently operates the winery.

The first thing you'll notice when you arrive is not the winery, but rather the specialty shops lining a path toward the tasting room. I was there during the Summer Expo, so I also saw country tap dancers as well as artists displaying their creations. The shops are open from 10 a.m. to 5 p.m. Tuesday through Sunday. They have a park and picnic area, and banquet and party facilities. There is also a farmer's market on Fridays from 9 a.m. to noon. The winery has a vineyard and also receives grapes from nearby Ramona and Temecula. There are many antique items on the property.

You can relax outside the tasting room under the covered patio and listen to laughter from people enjoying their tastings. The patio is near a soothing waterfall that could put you to sleep if you've had several glasses of wine. There are many plant and flower specimens throughout the winery.

While I was tasting wine inside at the tasting bar, a man spoke of his time during World War II. He said when he went through Normandy he tasted the wine there. He said the wine in Normandy had a much higher percentage of alcohol.

LOCATION: 13330 Paseo del Verano Norte, San Diego, California 92128
(858) 487-1866

 WEBSITE: www.Bernardowinery.com

 HOURS: 9 a.m. to 5 p.m. daily.

 TOURS: Available on request (guests may also walk through the winery and vineyards on their own).

 TASTING CHARGE: No cost for four samples of wine. Free crackers and popcorn are available. Cheese is available for a small charge.

 WINES AVAILABLE

White/Blush	Red	Also Available
Canelli	Barbera	Champagne
Chablis	Burgundy	Cream Sherry
Chardonnay	Cabernet Sauvignon	Light fruit wines
Gewürztraminer	California Chianti	Muscatel
Maddalena	Grenache	Non-alcoholic drinks
Vin Rosé	Merlot	Port
Vineyard Muscat	Syrah	
White Riesling		
White Zinfandel		

 DIRECTIONS: Take I-15 toward Rancho Bernardo to the Rancho Bernardo Road turnoff. Head east and make a left at Pomerado Road. At Paseo Del Verano Norte, make a right. From there, the winery is 1.5 miles and is on the right.

Deer Park Winery & Auto Museum

Deer Park Winery is located on 15 acres in the Escondido hills. As you walk through the gift shop you'll find the tasting area in the middle of the room. Deer Park's wines are produced in Escondido as well as at their sister winery in Napa Valley, which was established in 1891. The grounds are part of what makes a trip to this winery worthwhile. There's a creek bed with a foot bridge surrounded by a green lawn that looks like it's just begging for a bride and groom to be photographed there (wedding and reception sites are available).

Or, if you enjoy classic cars, you'll also want to make sure you visit this winery. There is a museum that features more than 100 classic automobiles.

The winery has picnic tables on the grounds; there's also an on-site deli, gift shop, market, and wine afficionado shop.

LOCATION: 29013 Champagne Boulevard, Escondido, California 92026
(760) 749-1666

 WEBSITE: www.deerparkwinery.com

 HOURS: 10 a.m. to 5 p.m. daily for tasting.
(Currently closed until mid-2004; call before visiting.)
(Last museum entry at 4 p.m.).

 TOURS: Self-guided.

 TASTING CHARGE: No charge for two tastes.

 WINES AVAILABLE

White	**Red**
Chardonnay	Cabernet Sauvignon
Muscat	Petite Sirah
Premium Cuvee (sparkling)	Zinfandel
Sauvignon Blanc	

 DIRECTIONS: Take I-15 to the Deer Springs/Mountain Meadow exit. Head east 1 block to Champagne Boulevard. Make a left. Deer Park Winery & Auto Museum is 3 miles north on the right.

Ferrara Winery

Ferrara Winery is a state historical point of interest (designated in 1971). The winery has been producing wine since 1932 and was started by George Ferrara. Currently his son Gasper operates the winery, which also has a picnic area on-site.

As I first walked into the tasting area I had flashbacks of my trip to Europe. The tasting room is old and dark, and if you can't get to Europe, this winery has a very similar atmosphere. The winery is very non-commercial and as I was walking toward the tasting room doors, I felt like I was walking on someone's private property. My companion and I were given two plastic (what looked like shot) glasses for tasting. After tasting four wines, we decided to check out the grounds. A group that had arrived a short time after us was visiting from Los Angeles and had made the trip to the winery specifically to purchase some marinade sauce they had remembered from long-ago family meals.

LOCATION: 1120 West 15th Avenue, Escondido, California 92025

(760) 745-7632

 WEBSITE: Not Available

 HOURS: 10 a.m. to 5 p.m. daily. Closed on Thanksgiving, Christmas, New Year's Day, and Easter.

 TOURS: Self-guided.

 TASTING: No charge.

 WINES AVAILABLE

White/Blush	Red	Also available
Chardonnay	Nebbiolo	Grape juice
Muscat of Alexandria		Wine marinade

 DIRECTIONS: Take I-15 toward Escondido to Ninth Avenue and head east to Upas Avenue. Make a right and drive south to 15th Avenue. Make a right. (The entrance looks like a residential driveway, but there are numerous signs to help guide you.)

Orfila Vineyards & Winery

Alejandro Orfila owns San Diego's largest winery. The winery sits on 30 acres near the San Diego Wild Animal Park. Orfila Winery changed names in the mid-1990s from "Thomas Jaeger Winery." Paul Thomas and the Jaeger family purchased the winery in 1988. Before that it was named "San Pasqual Winery." The grounds are beautiful and feature a picnic area surrounded by plants. The winery has an area for weddings and events and a grassy area with picnic tables overlooking the nearby golf course. Inside, you'll find a large tasting area in the middle of the room and along the walls you can find anything from T-shirts to olive oil to picnic foods such as French bread and cheese.

The winery has won numerous awards for their wines, including gold medals for their Gewürztraminer, Reserve Merlot, Pinot Noir, Sangiovese, Syrah, Zinfandel, and Tawny Port.

"We would love for San Diegans to think of us as one of the premier wineries in San Diego, but many people come to the winery after visiting the Wild Animal Park and they're not from here," said Leon Santoro, winemaker at Orfila Winery.

LOCATION: 13455 San Pasqual Road, Escondido, California 92025
(760) 738-6500

 WEBSITE: www.orfila.com

 HOURS: Open 10 a.m. to 6 p.m. daily except New Year's Day, Easter, July 4th, Thanksgiving, and Christmas.

 TOURS: Free 20-minute tours offered at 2 p.m. daily.

 TASTING: There is no charge to taste one wine. There is a $5 charge for a flight taste of five wines and includes a take-home glass.

 WINES AVAILABLE

White/Blush	**Red**	**Dessert**
Chardonnay	Merlot	Muscat Canelli
Gewürztraminer	Pinot Noir	Tawny Port
Viognier	Sangiovese	
White Riesling	Syrah	

 DIRECTIONS: Take I-15 toward Escondido and exit Via Rancho Parkway. Head east until you reach San Pasqual Road. Make a right. The winery is on the right, before the San Diego Wild Animal Park.

To see a world in a grain of sand
And heaven in a wild flower,
Hold infinity in the palm of your hand
And eternity in an hour.

- William Blake

Carlsbad

On a clear day you can see almost anything. That might be the best way to describe Carlsbad. East of Interstate 5 you will find the Carlsbad Company Stores, where you can enjoy shopping and have lunch at Bellefleur Restaurant. Quaint shops line the boulevard by the sea to the west of I-5, and among those shops you'll find Witch Creek Winery.

If you need a place to stay in Carlsbad, try the **Four Seasons Resort Aviara**. The phone number is (760) 603-6800, and the address is 7100 Four Seasons Point. You'll pay for the luxury of staying here but it's worth it if you can afford it. Amenities at this 5-star hotel include a golf course, spa, tennis courts, volleyball, and four restaurants. Some rooms offer views of Batiquitos Lagoon.

Closer to the coast and the wineries is the **Carlsbad Inn**. The inn is 100 yards from the beach and offers a pool, gym, game room, and sauna. The phone number is (800) 235-3939, and the address is 3075 Carlsbad Boulevard.

Bellefleur Restaurant

Bellefleur Restaurant is located near the Carlsbad Flower Fields, a 50-acre ranunculus field that blooms magnificently in spring. This winery has been in the making since the mid-1990s, and although they don't produce their wines on the premises (the winemaking is done in Fallbrook, about 20 miles northeast of Carlsbad), it is being mentioned here because they do have wine tastings at the bar. When the restaurant first opened, it included a demonstration vineyard near the entrance to the Carlsbad Company Stores mall, but the space has since been sold to retail outlets. The restaurant offers a room (featuring a long harvest table) for wine dinners and events. Customers can taste wine at the tables as well as at the bar.

LOCATION: 5610 Paseo del Norte, Carlsbad, California 92008
(760) 603-9861 (corporate office)
(760) 603-1919 (restaurant)

 WEBSITE: www.bellefleur.com

 HOURS: 11 a.m. to 9 p.m. daily, open until 10 p.m. on Friday and Saturday.

 TOURS: Not available.

 TASTING CHARGE: $5 for a flight of three white or red wines (at the bar, tables, or in the dining room). There is no charge for tasters.

 WINES AVAILABLE

White/Blush	**Red**
Chardonnay	Cabernet Sauvignon
Sauvignon Blanc	Merlot
White Zinfandel	

 DIRECTIONS: Take I-5 toward Carlsbad to the Palomar Airport Road offramp. Head east. Make a left at Paseo del Norte, which is the first traffic signal. Located inside the Carlsbad Company Stores mall.

Witch Creek Winery

Witch Creek Winery is a place to visit after a long day of shopping at the antique stores nearby or gazing at the waves crashing on the beach. The winery is close to Carlsbad Village, which has restaurants and antique stores on every corner.

The winery purchases grapes from various places throughout Southern California; oak barrels are stacked everywhere in the warehouse-like room. Witch Creek Winery opened in 1993, and is located on a busy street next to tourist-like shops. There are no acres of vines here. You'll find T-shirts with the winery's cat logo for sale and other wine gadgets inside. According to Dave Wodehouse, the owner, their tour-de-force is their large variety of red wines. Don't expect to find a lot of wineries nearby. Use this trip for shopping, lunch, and then an afternoon sip of wine.

LOCATION: 2906 Carlsbad Boulevard, Carlsbad, California 92008
(760) 720-7499

 WEBSITE: www.witchcreekwinery.com

 HOURS: 11 a.m. to 5 p.m. daily.

 TOURS: Available by appointment

 TASTING CHARGE: $3 (includes the glass).

 WINES AVAILABLE
The red wines are popular here. Varieties change.

White/Blush	Red	Dessert
Eye of Newt	Cabernet Sauvignon	Muscat Love
	Fat Cat Red	
	Nebbiolo	
	Merlot	
	Zinfandel	

 DIRECTIONS: Take I-5 toward Carlsbad to Carlsbad Village Drive. Head west. Make a right on Carlsbad Boulevard/Coast Highway. The winery is located on the corner of Grand Avenue and Carlsbad Boulevard on the right.

Witch Creek Winery House Recipe

Serve with their "Old Vine" Zinfandel.

French Beef Stew

Ingredients
1 lb quality stew meat
1 tbsp olive oil
1 large chopped brown onion
1 cup mushrooms
1 cup tomatoes (chopped)
2 cloves garlic
1/2 bottle of red wine
1 tbsp Italian seasonings
1 bay leaf
dash of salt and pepper

Brown the meat in the olive oil. Turn down the heat to a simmer and add the onion, garlic, mushrooms, tomatoes and red wine. Season with salt and pepper, Italian seasonings and bay leaf. Cover and simmer for 2–4 hours until tender. Serve with plain pasta or rice and steamed vegetables.

Ramona/Warner Springs

Ramona is an area that many San Diegans drive through in order to get to Julian. So if you are planning to go wine tasting in Julian, you may want to visit Schwaesdall Winery while you are in Ramona.

Warner Springs is located north of Julian. Shadow Mountain Vineyards is just past Warner Springs (the drive from Santa Ysabel is about a half hour). So you can also drive here if you're heading to Julian.

In the historic part of Ramona, look for **Ramona Vintners Cellars** at 632 Main Street, (760) 788-1388. They have a tasting room, a deli, and offer wines made from locally grown grapes. Also, **Eagle Gap Vineyards** has plans to eventually open a tasting room. They grow grapes for local wineries.

I recommend staying at one of the Julian B & Bs listed in the Julian section if you are planning to visit these wineries and need lodging.

Schwaesdall Winery

The excitement seems apparent at this young start-up winery. According to the owner, John Schwaesdall, the winery won a bronze medal for their 1997 Cabernet Sauvignon. Their tasting room is the first commercial straw-bale (the walls have straw inside, which is used for insulation) room in San Diego. Often, you will be greeted by John when you arrive. According to the winery's website, Schwaesdall began making wine from vineyards planted in Ramona in the 1950's.

The winery has about 4 acres of grapes in Ramona, and vineyards surrounding the tasting room. According to Schwaesdall, Ramona has the same climate as the Rhône Valley in France and in parts of Italy: he says that the Ramona Valley is known as the "Rhône Valley of California."

LOCATION: 17677 Rancho de Oro Road, Ramona, California 92065
(760) 789-7547

 WEBSITE: www.schwaesdallwinery.com

 HOURS: 10 a.m. to 6 p.m. weekends.

 TOURS: Self-guided.

 TASTING FEE: $5 for a taste of seven wines (take-home wineglass included).

 WINES AVAILABLE

Whites	**Reds**	**Dessert**
Chardonnay	Carignane	Muscat Cannelli
Sauvignon Blanc	Cabernet Sauvignon	
White Zinfandel	Merlot	
	Mourvèdre	
	Petite Sirah	
	Zinfandel	

 DIRECTIONS: Take I-8 east or Highway 78 east to Highway 67. Take Highway 67 to Schwaesdall Winery which is located right off of Highway 67 at Rancho de Oro Road (on the right hand side heading north, and the left hand side heading south).

Shadow Mountain Vineyards

The drive to Shadow Mountain Vineyards takes about 20 minutes from Santa Ysabel, according to owner Alex McGeary. The lazy drive started in Julian after I spent the night at Big Cat Cabin, a 1920's-era wood cabin surrounded by manzanita as well as evergreen and black oak trees. Once I got to Santa Ysabel, Highway 79 curved around an old mission, Lake Henshaw, and then into Warner Springs.

The entrance to Shadow Mountain Vineyards is marked by a beautiful sign (like those in Temecula or Napa Valley) and is located just off Highway 79. However, the facility is in the process of renovation; the drive up the winding dirt road was a little bumpy, but I could imagine that an entrance lined with Italian Cypress and rose bushes would add a stunning backdrop to the landscape.

I walked into the tiny tasting room, which is lined with magazine and newspaper articles about the winery and showcases Shadow Mountain's wine awards: two bronze medals for their Merlot from the Riverside International Competition and the Orange County Fair and a bronze medal from the San Diego National Wine Competition for their Cabernet Sauvignon. The attendant told me that their plans are to double the wine tasting area and add more gift products to the room. On display were quite a few watercolors painted by Alex's wife, Pamela. The winery boasts 60-year-old vines, although there is still talk of the fire that destroyed most of the estate in 1995. The vineyard consists of more than 30 acres of rolling hills, and the winery sells most of its wine through the tasting room. This is a mom-and-pop operation: Alex handles the vineyards and Pamela produces the labels for the bottles.

Although there is no restaurant on the grounds, occasionally the winery holds events catered by Pamela, who is also a gourmet chef. Talk about a multi-tasking couple! Alex attends many wine tasting events in San Diego in order to market their wine; he even works with local Warner Springs High School students to teach them the winemaking process.

LOCATION: 34680 Highway 79, Warner Springs, California 92086
(760) 782-0778

 WEBSITE: www.shadowmountainvineyard.com

 HOURS: 11 a.m. to 5 p.m. Wednesday through Sunday.

 TOURS: Call to arrange.

 TASTING CHARGE: $3 for a taste of nine wines (glass included).
There is no charge to taste if you're interested in a sample of just a few wines.

 WINES AVAILABLE

White/Blush	**Red**
Apple wine	Carignane/Mourvèdre
Chardonnay	Old Gus Red Rhône
Mountain Rosé	Syrah
Muscat	Zinfandel
Viognier	

 DIRECTIONS: From Santa Ysabel, take Highway 79 north toward Warner Springs. The winery is located on Highway 79, south of the Butterfield Stage route and 30 miles north of Julian. From Temecula, take I-15 south to Highway 76 east. Take Highway 79 north toward Warner Springs. The winery is located about 30 miles south of Temecula.

Julian

To residents of San Diego, Julian is as American as apple pie. Ask any San Diegan about Julian and they're bound to talk about the apple pie. The most popular time of year in Julian is the fall during the apple harvest. (The town can get very crowded at that time but a glimpse of the colorful fall leaves may be encouragement enough to brave the crowds.) Tourists crowd the streets in summer as well.

Some people in the area don't necessarily like the crowds, but they welcome them because they are beginning to realize that tourists are what make the town run. Some locals are pursuing ways to add more parking areas, picnic tables, and restaurants to make the town more friendly to visitors.

Julian is surrounded by Volcan Mountain and the Cuyamaca Mountains. The community dates back to 1869 when gold was first discovered there. Today, you can still pan for gold at one of the booths along the town's center on Main Street.

The area's founding father was Drue Bailey, a former soldier. He, along with his brother, Frank Bailey, and cousins Webb and Mike Julian, were heading to Arizona when they stopped to rest in what is now the area of Julian. Drue liked the area so much that he and his companions ended up staying. Frank decided to continue to Arizona but returned in 1870 when he heard of the gold discovery. The town's name comes from Mike Julian, Bailey's cousin.

Julian's first apple orchards were planted in the 1870s by Thomas Brady. The demand for apple pie keeps apple growers busy; apple trees are everywhere in Julian. Almost no one leaves the area without trying a piece of apple pie or drinking some cider. Although Julian is most famous for its apples, the area has a little-known secret. It's called Menghini Winery and a trip to Julian wouldn't be complete without visiting this mom-and-pop delight.

Look for **Orfila Winery's** tasting room located at 4470 Highway 78, Julian, (760) 765-0102. Their website is www.orfila.com. Generally, you'll see it as you're driving into town if you take Highway 78.

Julian Chamber of Commerce
(760) 765-1857
www.julianca.com

Note: As the second edition of this book is completed, the largest forest fire in San Diego's history had recently threatened Julian. Many homes and businesses in nearby Cuyamaca were destroyed and lives were lost. Firefighters were determined to save the historic mining town, and did save it, but sadly one died in the fire.

Also, unfortunately some of the places to stay that were included in the previous edition of this book are no longer standing including the Artist's Loft, Big Cat Cabin and Strawberry Hill. The owners of these cabins had remodeled them with their own hands and had quit their jobs to build their dream home nearby. They not only lost their home, but also their business. This is just one example of the fire's destruction.

Places to Stay

Julian Bed and Breakfast Guild

(760) 765-1555

This guild is a network of bed and breakfast providers. They offer a directory with information about each participating property. All guild members are listed with the Automobile Club (AAA). Following is information about each of the inns of the guild (all offer breakfast). Call for rates.

Butterfield

(800) 379-4262

Offers five rooms: two of which have fireplaces, and one is a cottage. Each has private bathroom. There are candlelit dinners available for guests. Within walking distance of downtown Julian.

LeeLin Wikiup

(800) 6-WIKIUP

Offers two large suites with queen-size beds and bathrooms, wet bars, and separate entries. Also has a room with a king-size feather bed and bath in the main house. There is a common area that features a fireplace, TV, VCR, and game table. Children and dogs are welcome.

Orchard Hill Country Inn

(800) 71 ORCHARD (716-7242)

Located near downtown Julian, this inn has won attention and awards including one from *Country Inns Magazine* for the 1996 Waverly Inn of the Year, and was given 4 stars by AAA.

Rockin' A

(760) 765-2820

Offers three rooms. Two of the rooms have their own entrances, bathrooms, and fireplaces. The other room is located in the main house and has a bathroom with a jet tub. Features include 5.5 acres with farm animals, fruit orchards, fishing pond, pool, and spa. Apple pie and cider are served in the afternoon.

Shadow Mountain Ranch

(760) 765-0323

Offers themed cottages and rooms in main house. Unique features include afternoon tea service, a lap pool, hot tub, archery, badminton, croquet, and horseshoes.

Mountain High

(760) 765-1083

Offers a cottage that has a kitchen, private deck, living room, and TV/VCR. Also offers a room with its own entry and patio garden, fireplace, bathroom, and TV. Unique features include a gazebo and Jacuzzi.

Pinecroft Manor

(760) 765-1611

Offers two rooms with one bathroom to share. Also offers three cabins with kitchens that accommodate between two and fourteen people. Unique features include five-level English Tudor home with antiques and English gardens. Children are welcome. Refreshments are served in the afternoon.

Eagle Nest

(760) 765-1252

Offers three guest rooms, one with private bath. One of the rooms with a shared bath has a fireplace. Unique features include a modern Victorian home with antique furnishings and swimming pool. Allows children but not pets.

Directions to Julian

From San Diego take I-8 east or Highway 78 east to Highway 79.
The main town of Julian is located on Highway 79 (about a 90-minute
drive from San Diego).

J. Jenkins Winery

I recently spoke with Jim Jenkins, of J. Jenkins Winery, about his new establishment in Julian (just a stone's throw away from Menghini Winery), and here's what he had to say:

Janene Roberts: What made you decide to start a winery in Julian?

Jim Jenkins: I wanted a winery for 30 years. While I was practicing medicine, I used to come to Julian on the weekends to visit my friends, the Menghinis. I fell in love with the valley. I purchased some property here 5 years ago. I've basically been making wine for 30 years.

JR: What kind of grapes do you grow?

JJ: I grow Pinot Grigio and Pinot Noir on-site in Julian. I have 10 acres: 8 acres are apple trees; the vineyard is a 1/2 acre. I didn't know if grapes would do well. The Pinot Grigio is doing well; we sold out of it 4 months ago. I have friends in San Diego who have 2 acres of Syrah. I purchased grapes from them for 2 years. I also purchased Merlot from Temecula. I make apple wines. Two to three wines are raised on the property. In Julian we have Pinot Grigio, Pinot Noir, Merlot, Muscat Canelli, Sauvignon Blanc, and Cabernet Sauvignon. They are small-acreage growers. No one wanted to put in large amounts of grapes. The bottom line is people are trying to raise grapes here. We're trying to find out what we can and cannot raise.

JR: Do you have a viticultural background?

JJ: I've been to [U.C.] Davis; I took courses in enology. Some of my friends are winemakers. We trade war stories. There is an amateur winemaking group in San Diego; I was the president for 2 years. There are about 40 to 45 people in it. Lots of people in San Diego make home wines.

JR: What are your dreams for the future?

JJ: In 2 months we're building a winery that's also a production facility on the property. We're currently working in what was the office. We're going to put the tasting room in there (the new production facility).

 LOCATION: 1255 Julian Orchards Drive, P.O. Box 2094 Julian, California 92036
(760) 765-3267

 WEBSITE: Not Available.

 HOURS: Saturday and Sunday, from 11 a.m. to 5 p.m.

 TOURS: By appointment.

 TASTING CHARGE: $3 for the wine tasting (tasters receive a logo-imprinted glass).

 WINES AVAILABLE: The winery tries to produce niche market wines that others aren't producing like their Nouveau, which is produced in the traditional manner.

White	Red
Apple Wine	Merlot
Pinot Grigio	Nouveau
	Pinot Noir
	Syrah

 DIRECTIONS: From Highway 79 in Julian continue on Highway 79 headed north. After you leave Main Street the highway turns into Farmers Road. Make a left at Julian Orchards Drive.

Menghini Winery

When you arrive at the winery, don't make the mistake of thinking the plants surrounding it are grapevines–they are actually apple trees. Silver tags are attached to the trees to keep the birds away. According to Toni Menghini, the winery is starting to grow more of their own grapes.

As we drove up the dirt road to the tasting room, we parked next to a Lexus. We walked into the tasting area where two lazy dogs snoozed on the floor. The temperature was cool inside–a nice respite from the August heat. We looked around the room at some of the wares for sale. One item that caught my attention was the Menghini apple wine. Once we began talking to the wine host, we were delighted by the pleasantness of the staff and the casualness of the owners. The winey is owned by a husband and wife team named Michael and Toni Menghini.

We were offered an apple from their basket. The apples were about the size of plums and green and very sweet. They even asked us to take some home.

In the back of the tasting room and among the apple trees is a Bed and Wine, a new concept (Toni Menghini said it'd be hard to offer breakfast when they're not around in the morning). People who stay there may chose a bottle of wine and an assortment of cheeses to take with them to their room.

The winery has various events including an art show in the fall featuring music, a country barbeque, and wine tasting. There is also a Julian grape stomp. The winery has a picnic area with tables for seasonal use.

LOCATION: 1150 Julian Orchards Drive, Julian, California 92036
(760) 765-2072

 WEBSITE: Not Available

 HOURS: 10 a.m. to 4 p.m. weekdays and 10 a.m. to 5 p.m. weekends. (10 a.m. to 4 p.m. daily in the winter.)

 TOURS: By appointment only.

 TASTING CHARGE: No charge.

 WINES AVAILABLE

White/Blush	Red
Apple wine (Mela)	Cabernet Sauvignon
Chardonnay	Merlot
Julian Blossom	
Muscat Canelli (Julian Gold)	
Sauvignon Blanc	

 DIRECTIONS: From Highway 79 in Julian continue on Highway 79 headed north. After you leave Main Street the highway turns into Farmers Road. Make a left at Julian Orchards Drive.

Witch Creek

Witch Creek in Julian is a place for tasting only. It opened in 1984, but you won't find vineyards here; their wines are brought from their Carlsbad winery of the same name.

 LOCATION: 2000 Main Street, Suite 106 and 107, Julian, California 92036
(760) 765-2023

 WEBSITE: www.witchcreekwinery.com

 HOURS: 11 a.m. to 5 p.m. weekdays and 10 a.m. to 5 p.m. weekends.

 TOURS: Not available.

 TASTING CHARGE: $3 (take-home glass included).

 WINES AVAILABLE

White/Blush	**Red**
Chenin Blanc	Cabernet Sauvignon
Eye of Newt with 1%	Merlot
Grenache	Reserve (Rhône Valley style)
	Tempranillo
	Zinfandel

 DIRECTIONS: Located in downtown Julian on Main Street.

Witch Creek House Recipe

You may want to serve this dish with one of their Rhône blends such as "La Mariage." The winery suggests accompanying the pork with plain rice and a vegetable.

Roast Pork Loin with Mushroom Sauce

Ingredients
1 boneless or boned pork loin
1 cup cream sherry
1/2 cup minced red onions
4 tbsp butter
1 cup fresh, diced mushrooms
1/2 cup port
1 handful fresh cilantro

Roast the pork loin. Deglaze the roasting pan with the cream sherry. In a sauce pan, sauté the red onions in the butter. Add the mushrooms, the port, and the mixture from the deglazed pork pan. Cover the pan and adjust the heat to medium-high. This will cook the mushrooms quickly. Once the mushrooms are tender, but have retained their shape, remove the lid and turn the heat to high. The mixture will reduce and thicken in about 5 minutes. Make sure you watch and stir the ingredients. Once the mixture has thickened, add the cilantro and immediately serve over the pork loin.

Wineries of Temecula

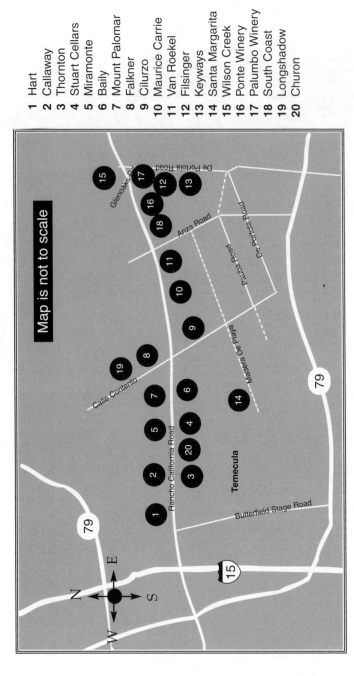

Map is not to scale

1 Hart
2 Callaway
3 Thornton
4 Stuart Cellars
5 Miramonte
6 Baily
7 Mount Palomar
8 Falkner
9 Cilurzo
10 Maurice Carrie
11 Van Roekel
12 Filsinger
13 Keyways
14 Santa Margarita
15 Wilson Creek
16 Ponte Winery
17 Palumbo Winery
18 South Coast
19 Longshadow
20 Churon

Wineries of Temecula

Temecula is becoming a very prominent winery area. Beginning in the '80s, Temecula boasted more wineries than the Cucamonga district to the north. The first plantings of vineyards in Temecula began in the 1960s with the help of the University of California at Davis, currently a main center for wine science. Hart Winery, Cilurzo, and Callaway wineries were some of the first in the area. By 1981 there were 3,000 acres of vineyards in Temecula. Now, there are 20 wineries and more keep sprouting up all the time. Temecula's climate is often compared to the Mediterranean. Grape vines are planted in a basin 23 miles from the Pacific Ocean. The area receives cool, damp sea air from the ocean breezes that flow in through an open space in the west hills. This opening cools the valley enough to grow wine grapes. At night, cool air also keeps the temperature under control. The convenience of irrigation water helps vines grow here as well.

For most of Temecula's history, the wineries have been trying to grow the Napa and Sonoma Valley grape varieties such as Chardonnay. Only recently have they realized that it would be better to plant grapes that are more favorable to their climate, specifically, Italian grapes. Both Hart and Mount Palomar wineries in the Temecula area have produced Sangiovese, a red grape from Chianti, Italy. So far, the results have been impressive and some of the wineries have won awards for the Italian varietal wines. Other new varietals being produced in the area are Mourvèdre and Nebbiolo.

The Temecula Valley's predominant varietal is still Chardonnay, however Merlot is also showing some growth. Today, the area around Rancho California Road is really developing. Most of Temecula's residential and commercial development is centered around the winery area.

Directions to Temecula

Take I-15 toward Temecula to the Rancho California Road exit. Head east on Rancho California Road. The wineries are approximately 70 miles from San Diego.

Heading east on Rancho California Road, there's an Embassy Suites hotel to the right and a shopping mall across the street. At the first intersection is an office called Rancho California Temecula Information Center Real Estate, which offers free information. It's a great place to stop before heading to the wineries.

As you drive toward the wineries, the real estate center is located at the first light after the freeway offramp, which is Ynez Road. Make a left. It's on the corner of Rancho California Road and Ynez. The office provides free maps of the area.

After crossing Ynez you'll find a road sign welcoming you to the wine country. You'll see this about 4 miles east of the freeway. Most of the wineries are located on Rancho California Road.

> Tip: Contact an Auto Club office near you and ask them for a Temecula Winery package.

Our first trip to Temecula began with the Hart Winery. Four hours and six wineries later, our parched lips and weary bodies were ready to head home. Of the six wineries we visited (Hart, Baily, Callaway, Thornton, Maurice Carrie, and Mount Palomar) only Hart Winery offered wine tasters crackers. We noticed a lot of people buying French bread at Mount Palomar Winery and recommend that tasters do the same; we headed home craving bread or crackers.

Hotels/Bed and Breakfast Inns

Embassy Suites
29345 Rancho California Road, Temecula, California 92591
(909) 676-5656 or 1 (800) EMBASSY
You can't miss this hotel. You'll see it as soon as you exit the freeway.

Loma Vista Bed & Breakfast
33350 La Serena Way, Temecula, California 92591
(909) 676-7047
Located in the heart of the winery area overlooking grape vines.

Temecula Creek Inn
44501 Rainbow Canyon Road, Temecula, California 92592
(909) 694-1000 or 1 (800) 962-7335
Has a 27-hole golf course and tennis courts.

Comfort Inn
27338 Jefferson Avenue, Temecula, California 92590
(909) 296-3788 or 1 (800) 221-2222
Has an outdoor pool, continental breakfast, and a 2-star rating from AAA. Ask about AAA discounts.

Best Western Country Inn
27706 Jefferson Avenue, Temecula, California 92590
(909) 676-7378 or 1 (800) 528-1234
Offers a continental breakfast, heated outdoor swimming pool, and sauna.

Rodeway Inn

28718 Front Street, Temecula, California 92590

(909) 676-4833

Has a pool and spa and is located about 3.5 miles from the wineries.

Inn at Churon Winery

33233 Rancho California Road, Temecula, California 92591

(909) 694-9070

Temecula Springs Resort

34843 Rancho California Road, Temecula, California 92591

(909) 587-9463

Limo Tours

A number of limousine companies offer tours to the Temecula Valley.

Top Cat Limousine

(858) 546-7550

Offers five-hour winery tours. Call for reservations. You can rent a limo for six people. The driver will pick you up anywhere in San Diego and drive you to the wineries. The limo is stocked with ice and glasses; guests are also welcome to bring drinks and snacks. They'll decorate the car (at no extra cost) for special occasions. Total cost does not include driver's gratuity.

Paul The Greek Limousine

(619) 589-2299

Offers six-hour tours. The limo company claims to have $75,000 cars and the nicest limousines in town–with mirrors and lights on the ceiling.

Grapeline Wine Country Shuttle

This is a van tour (holds about 20 passengers) through the Temecula winery area. Tours and packages available.

(888) 8WINERY www.gogrape.com

Temecula Valley Vintners Association
(909) 699-3626 or 1 (800) 801-9463.
Call to request a brochure about the wine country.

A Stay at Loma Vista Bed & Breakfast

At first blush the Loma Vista Bed & Breakfast Inn appears to be like a large home, and it is in a sense. The owners live on the premises, and the living room features an old-fashioned-looking television (like one you'd find at mom's). There's a large dining table where they have the most sumptuous breakfast for guests at 9 a.m. When I visited, the breakfast consisted of a starter of a smoothie-type strawberry-flavored concoction in a martini glass, followed by a ham and chicken blintz and a warm croissant. Champagne, juice, and coffee were also served, and at the end they brought out small round brownies dusted with confectioners sugar. The breakfast was the highlight for me. Not only was the food good, but the discussions with all the other guests couldn't be beat. I left with four business cards and a feeling of having been at a Thanksgiving dinner. The inn offers 10 rooms (all with different names) that overlook vineyards, and they have a Jacuzzi near the garden, which is full of roses, geraniums, and various herbs and shrubs.

Baily Vineyard & Winery

This winery's new stone building with vines growing along the walls looks as though it might be a tasting room in Europe or Napa Valley. Their gift shop features lots of gargoyles and you'll find them in Carol's Restaurant, as well as on the outside of the building. They have a demonstration garden you'll see as you walk toward the tasting room.

The winery began in 1986 by a former computer software developer, his wife, and their two sons. The owners, Phil and Carol Baily, operate not only Baily Vineyard & Winery but also Carol's Restaurant. There's also a separate gift shop that has unique items for sale. Occasionally winemaker dinners are offered featuring special menus that enhance local wines. Carol's is next door to the winery and features a fireplace and warm atmosphere.

I had lunch at Carol's one December afternoon. I was seated in front of the fireplace in the gargoyle-ensconced, European-influenced restaurant alone, but this restaurant made me feel empowered to do it, and it felt intimate to be sitting in front of the fireplace surrounded by other diners as if I might be eating at a really nice home. I had a glass of their '99 Merlot, which garnered an 88 in *Wine Spectator's* listing, and ordered a chicken and gouda croissant sandwich.

LOCATION: Tasting Room
33440 La Serena, Temecula, California 92591
(909) 676-9463

 WEBSITE: www.bailywinery.com

 TASTING ROOM HOURS: 11 a.m. to 5 p.m. Monday - Friday
and Sunday; Saturday 10 a.m. to 5 p.m.

 TOURS: Not available

 TASTING CHARGE: $5 to taste five wines (includes take-
home glass), $10 to taste premium reds.

 WINES AVAILABLE

White/Blush	**Red**	**Dessert**
Chardonnay	Cabernet Sauvignon	Late Harvest
Muscat Blanc	Merlot	
Riesling	Sangiovese	
Sémillon-Sauvignon	Meritage	
Blanc (Blend)		

 DIRECTIONS: To get to the tasting room, take I-15, exit at
Rancho California Road, and head east. The winery will be on
the right.

Callaway Coastal Winery

Callaway recently changed its name from "Callaway Vineyard & Winery" to "Callaway Coastal Winery" in a nod to where they're getting some of their grapes from–the coastal areas of Santa Barbara, Paso Robles, and Monterey County. The move helps Callaway reduce some of the prices of their wine and follows in the footsteps of Robert Mondavi Coastal and BV Coastal.

You'll enjoy the rosebush-lined drive to the winery that was founded by Ely Callaway in 1969; flowers seem to be everywhere.

A greeter in the front of the winery takes reservations for complimentary winery tours and will sell you wine tasting tickets. The winery's tasting fees include a take-home glass. The tour explains the winemaking process at Callaway from harvest to bottling.

The picnic area is a great place for lunch. It is next to the winery and if you walk over to a stone ledge near the parking lot, you get a broad view of the vines. The picnic area is equipped with mist sprayers that keep you cool in hot weather. During the middle of the summer, temperatures can reach into the low 100s. If you want to buy lunch, Allie's at Callaway offers lunch and dinner. The menu specializes in California-Mediterranean cuisine.

Private group events are available including tours, wine tasting, and luncheons (advance reservations required). The winery also holds special wine and food events throughout the year. Call the winery for more information.

LOCATION: 32720 Rancho California Road, Temecula, California 92589
(909) 676-4001 or 1 (800) 472-2377

 WEBSITE: www.callawaycoastal.com

 HOURS: 10 a.m. to 5 p.m. daily.

 TOURS: Weekdays at 11 a.m., 1 p.m., and 3 p.m. and every hour on the hour on weekends.

 TASTING CHARGE: $5 for four wines (includes a take-home glass).

 WINES AVAILABLE

White/Blush	**Red**	**Dessert**
Chardonnay	Cabernet Sauvignon	Muscat Canelli
Chenin Blanc	Dolcetto	
Pinot Gris	Merlot	
Sauvignon Blanc		
Viognier		

 DIRECTIONS: Take I-15 to the Rancho California Road exit. Head east for about 4 miles. The winery is on the left.

Churon Winery/
The Inn at Churon Winery

I thought I had booked a room at The Inn at Churon Winery in Temecula to "find myself." What I found instead was the spirit of the people of Temecula and their willingness to fight for their dreams.

My journey began with a check-in on a Sunday afternoon. The winery was practically deserted, probably because it was the weekend before Christmas and people were most likely taking care of last-minute holiday preparations.

I stayed in one of the vineyard-view rooms. My room had a huge marble-covered bathroom with a large spa tub (big enough for two, according to inn staff) and separate shower area.

The room's fireplace could be started by the switch of a timer. The bed was large, probably a king, and had wonderfully soft cotton linens and a down-filled comforter. The furnishings were French inspired and French doors opened to a view of the vineyards. A minor complaint: the room faced Rancho California Road, which is slightly noisy at night and thus I didn't use the French doors. The room was decorated in neutrals with touches of yellow and blues.

At about 5:30 p.m. I went down to the Inn's tasting room for the wine reception. There were only three people in the expansive room: a young couple (probably in their 20s) and the wine attendant. There were crackers and cheese on the counter with slices of cheddar, swiss, gorgonzola, and a wheel of brie with baguettes. The wine attendant made me feel right at home. She asked me if I was alone. I told her I was, and I could tell from her look that she was wondering why. She asked if I was traveling for business or pleasure; I told her both. The young couple came over to the counter and the attendant smoothly included them into the conversation and then proceeded to tell stories about the area.

A new winery just opened up off of Rancho California Road, she said. A young man in his 30s opened it; he has a sign on a wine barrel out front that says "Wine Tasting." You'll see it–it's just off the main road. The young couple, engaged to be married at the time, offered that someone else in the area was planning to open a resort. They said the resort owner expected that it would take only a year to be opened. The wine attendant said that it had taken The Inn at Churon 6 or 7 years to open because of all the permits and red tape; it could take years for the new resort to be completed (they were referring to Temecula Springs Resort).

But the new resort is starting. You can see the frame of buildings and the land scaled and ready. Maybe Temecula is a land of dreams, a light in someone's eye–like an unborn child. They see it in their mind first, that glimmer. Maybe it's about the tenacity of the dreamer. Just stick it out for 6 or 7 years, just to start, never mind the amount of time needed to turn a profit. I don't think many of these people are in it for the profit. It's the love of the land, or the romantic dream of living among vineyards, the fog in the morning rolling through the valley as they sip their morning coffee. Maybe it's their pioneer spirit, their faith that one day they will be taken seriously, that keeps prodding them along. And people in Temecula–especially the vintners–must be eternal optimists. They're plowing through Pierce's disease, through never-ending home developments, through practically unimaginable traffic, and through the naysayers who scoff at the quality of their wines (even after they score 80s and 90s in *Wine Spectator's* listings, or continue to win medals in the latest fair competitions).

These people aren't ready to give up. So they buy the land, and wait the many years before their dreams become a reality, and pretty soon the naysayers, the critics, start coming around. They start drinking the wines and staying at the inns. As they sip their gold-medal wines, the critics somehow forget that 5 to 10 years ago, they claimed that this valley would never amount to anything. Fair-weather fans always cheer for teams when they're on top. But they forget about the pioneers, the ones with the gleam in their eyes.

The pioneers knew all along. They could see the rolling hills blessed with Italian Cypress trees and warm soil, and it reminded them of the hills of Italy. They realized how, in the mornings and nights, the cold chills would help the grape vines. The pioneers were both dreamers and doers: they tended to the sick grape vines and brought them back to health–more vigorous than ever.

This is what makes Temecula a thriving place. The can-do spirit of the people–like the settlers of America. The vintners won't quit when diseased vines wreck havoc on their businesses; they'll just rebuild–and have stories to tell their grandkids.

I see the gleam in the eyes of the wine attendant and the couple standing next to me at the Inn. We're the believers. I spent that night trying to discover myself, but realized that really we're not all that different. We all want to pursue our dreams, and hope that someone else shares those dreams with us. So the critics' voices won't matter as you plow through the murk together, always seeing that light, knowing that the dream will eventually become a reality–boring paperwork, permits and all.

LOCATION: 33233 Rancho California Road, Temecula, California 92591 (909) 694-9070

 WEBSITE www.innatchuronwinery.com

 TASTING HOURS: Daily from 10:00 a.m. to 5 p.m.

 TOURS: Not available.

 **TASTING CHARGE:** $5 for five tastings including a free glass.

 WINES AVAILABLE:

White	Red
Chardonnay	Cabernet Sauvignon
Chenin Blanc meritage	Merlot
Viognier	Nebbiolo
	Syrah

DIRECTIONS: Take I-15 to the Rancho California Road exit. Head east. The winery and inn are on the right side, after Thornton Winery.

A night's stay includes a full breakfast in the morning and a wine reception in the evening. The tasting room is spacious with numerous gifts and a sweeping staircase leads you to the reception room of the inn.

Cilurzo Vineyard & Winery

Cilurzo Vineyard & Winery was one of the first wineries in the Valley and the owners, Vincenzo and Audrey Cilurzo, like to say that the vineyard was planted in 1968 B.C. (Before Callaway). The winery wasn't built until 10 years later, in 1978, when they had their first grape crush.

At this winery you can taste up to eight different wines for $2–probably the best deal in the Temecula Valley besides the wineries that have free tastings and although the winery's tasting room isn't brand new, the friendly staff should be encouragement enough to stop by.

The winery's picnic area overlooks a lake. Snack and gift items are for sale and group catering is available. The winery also has barrel tastings and dinner events. You can rent the winery's hilltop adobe home and poolside patio for luncheons, dinners, banquets, and barbecues.

The winery received a double gold (Best of Class) for the 1998 Reserve Petit Sirah at the California State Fair Wine Competition.

LOCATION: 41220 Calle Contento, Temecula, California 92592
(909) 676-5250

 WEBSITE: www.cilurzowine.com

 HOURS: 10 a.m. to 5 p.m. daily.

 TOURS: By appointment only.

 TASTING CHARGE: $2 to taste eight wines.

 WINES AVAILABLE

White/Blush	**Red**
Chardonnay	Cabernet Sauvignon
Chenin Blanc	Late Harvest Petite Sirah
Muscat Canelli	Merlot Reserve
Sauvignon Blanc	Petite Sirah
Viognier	Vincheno
Zinfandel Rose	(a red and white mix)
	Zinfandel

 DIRECTIONS: Take I-15 to Rancho California Road and head east about 5 miles. Make a right on Calle Contento. The winery is located on Calle Contento.

Falkner Winery

Falkner Winery, formally Temecula Crest Winery, sits at the top of a hill and has kept the look of Temecula Crest but has added more features such as an outdoor wine tasting area overlooking a grassy field and a lunch menu.

The winery's wood structure would fit well in the mountains and inside the tasting area you feel like you perhaps had made the long drive there. They offer wine classes like "Introduction to Wine" and "Advanced Tasting," and on Sunday afternoons have free jazz.

The winery also offers wedding packages that include everything from the space overlooking mountains, vineyards, and valleys to an unlimited-consumption beverage package, a wine club, and special events throughout the year. Call the winery for more information.

The *Wine Enthusiast* rated their '99 Amante a 93, and their 200 Sauvignon Blanc an 86 out of 100.

LOCATION: 40620 Calle Contento, Temecula, California 92591
(909) 676-8231

 WEBSITE: www.falknerwinery.com

 HOURS: Daily 10 a.m. to 5 p.m.

 TOURS: 11 a.m (free) and 2 p.m ($3) every weekend.

 TASTING CHARGE: $5 to taste five wines (includes a take-home glass).

 WINES AVAILABLE

White/Blush	**Red**	**Dessert**
Chardonnay	Cabernet Sauvignon	Muscat Canelli
Fume Blanc	Cello	Port
Riesling	Meritage	
Sauvignon Blanc	Merlot	
Super Tuscan	Syrah	
"Amante"		
Viognier		

 DIRECTIONS: Take I-15 and exit at Rancho California Road. Head east. Calle Contento is a cross street of Rancho California Road. Make a left at Calle Contento. The winery is on the right.

Filsinger Vineyards & Winery

For a winery that wants to hide out from the crowd in the Temecula area, it does a poor job because it provides quality wines and a down-to-earth approach to wine tasting. Filsinger Vineyards & Winery began in 1980 by Dr. Bill Filsinger, Kathy Filsinger, and Eric Filsinger, (the assistant winemaker).

The winery doesn't search out wine tasters, but wine tasters should search out the winery. The Filsinger family has roots in Germany, and had a winery there before World War II. They decided to start a winery in Temecula in the German tradition, and they claim to be one of the first wineries in Southern California to grow and produce Gerwürtztraminer.

You'll find a picnic area and gift items available here; a banquet room and a kitchen that seats 45–50 people are also available for rent.

LOCATION: 39050 De Portola Road, Temecula, California 92592

(888) 434-5746 or (909) 302-6363

WEBSITE: www.filsingerwinery.com

HOURS: 10 a.m. to 5 p.m. weekends.
             11 a.m. to 4 p.m. Fridays.

TOURS: By appointment only.

TASTING CHARGE: $2 for a taste of five wines.

WINES AVAILABLE

White/Blush	**Red**	**Dessert**
Chardonnay	Cabernet Sauvignon	Late Harvest
Fumé Blanc	Nebbiolo	Zinfandel
Gerwürtztraminer	Sparkling	
Muscat Orange		
Riesling		
Sauvignon Blanc		
White Zinfandel		

DIRECTIONS: Head east on Rancho California Road and make a right on Glenoaks Road (Glenoaks Road is about 10 miles from I-15). Make a right on De Portola Road.

Hart Winery

Hart Winery's building looks like a place you might find in the Old West. But it's not from that era; the winery was started in 1980.

The tasting room is located in a small building with a porch in the front that looks as though it's waiting for some horses to be tied to it. The tasting room is refrigerator-cold inside but the number of people who pack into the little room will keep you warm. Don't miss this winery. Its unpretentious look makes you feel right at home. This winery specializes in red wines.

The *Wall Street Journal* named Hart Winery's rosé wine one of its favorite brands. The newspaper found only three rosés in America that were "excellent," one of those bottles came from Hart Winery. It turns out Hart Winery's Grenache Rosé wine wins awards every year at the Los Angeles County Fair. You'll probably have to visit the winery in order to purchase a bottle because the wines are produced on a limited basis.

Their 1998 Syrah won a gold medal at the Monterey Wine Competition and they also won a gold for their 2000 Grenache Rosé at the Pacific Rim International Wine Competition.

A small picnic area is available.

LOCATION: 41300 Avenida Biona, Temecula, California 92591
(909) 676-6300

 WEBSITE: Not Available.

 TASTING HOURS: 9 a.m. to 4:30 p.m. daily.

 TOURS: Available on request for large groups.

 TASTING CHARGE: $5 (includes a take-home glass).

 WINES AVAILABLE

White/Blush	**Red**
Fumé Blanc	Cabernet Franc
Grenache Rosé	Merlot
Viognier	Mourvèdre
	Proprietary
	Syrah
	Zinfandel

 DIRECTIONS: From I-15, exit Rancho California Road. Go east. It's the first winery on the left. Avenida Biona is actually the winery's driveway.

Keyways Vineyard & Winery

Keyways Vineyard & Winery is a place for people who love wine and antiques. The winery, which was opened in 1988 by Carl Key, sells most of its wine from the winery. Key recently sold the winery and although the current owners plan on keeping the name and the look for now, they may change it in the future.

The winery has a view overlooking vineyards and an area where you can ride and tie up horses. (You'll have to provide your own horse, though.)

LOCATION: 37338 De Portola Road, Temecula, California 92592
(909) 302-7888

 WEBSITE: Not available.

 HOURS: 10 a.m. to 5 p.m. daily.

 TOURS: Not available.

 TASTING CHARGE: $5 for a taste of seven to nine wines.

 WINES AVAILABLE
The vintner recommends their Zinfandel.

White/Blush	Red	Dessert
Chardonnay	Cabernet Franc	Muscat
Riesling	Cabernet Sauvignon	
Sauvignon Blanc	Petite Syrah	
Viognier	Zinfandel	

 DIRECTIONS: Take I-15 to Rancho California Road east. Make a right at Glenoaks Road and a right at De Portola Road. The winery is located just after Filsinger Winery.

Long Shadow Ranch Winery

Surrounded by horses and white ranch-style fencing, Long Shadow Ranch Winery sits along a dirt road right after Falkner Winery. Here you'll find a park-like setting with picnic tables near horse stables; a white carriage sits on the grass-covered area. The tasting room is small and intimate, and reminds me of a tasting room you might find tucked into a corner of Sonoma Valley.

Perhaps this winery's distinction is in its offering of horse-drawn carriage wine tasting trips. Their Belgian draft horses will take you through vineyards around Temecula.

LOCATION: 39847 Calle Contento, Temecula, California 92591
(909) 587-6221

 WEBSITE: www.Longshadowranch.net

 HOURS: Friday through Sunday 10 a.m. to 5 p.m.

 TOURS: Not available, but offers carriage tours around the vineyards a couple hours each day on the weekends.

 TASTING CHARGE: $5 for five tastings (includes glass).

 WINES AVAILABLE:

White/Blush	Red	Dessert
Chardonnay	Sangiovese	Muscat
Sauvignon Blanc	Merlot	
White Grenache		

 **DIRECTIONS:** Take I-15 toward Temecula, exit at Rancho California Road heading east. Make a left at Calle Contento.

Maurice Carrie Winery

I like to say that Maurice Carrie is the Southern Belle of the Temecula wineries. Maybe it's the gazebo and rose bushes out front—or perhaps it's the friendly people. Or it could be the bustling atmosphere inside. Started in 1986 by Maurice and Bud Van Roekel, the winery is comfortable and makes you feel right at home. The vineyard was started with the Van Roekel's planting grapes in 1968. They established the first vineyard in the region. By 1986, they built the Victorian-era style winery, and currently sell about 25,000 cases of wine annually.

There's lots of merchandise for sale in addition to the wine. Deli items include sourdough bread baked on the premises (one type has brie baked inside). There is also a picnic area.

LOCATION: 34225 Rancho California Road, Temecula, California 92591
(909) 676-1711

 WEBSITE: www.mauricecarriewinery.com

 HOURS: 10 a.m. to 5 p.m. daily.

 TOURS: Tours are available for fifteen or more people when reservations are made in advance.

 TASTING CHARGE: Complimentary.

WINES AVAILABLE

White /Blush	Red	Dessert
Chardonnay	Cabernet Sauvignon	Late Harvest
Riesling	Merlot	Muscat Canelli
Sauvignon Blanc		
White Zinfandel		

 DIRECTIONS: Take I-15 and exit at Rancho California Road. Head east on Rancho California Road. The winery is about 6 miles from the freeway on the right side.

Miramonte Winery

Miramonte is located atop a hill overlooking vineyards and is housed in a warehouse-looking building. But don't be fooled by the outward appearance. Inside you'll find a cool, open, and large wine tasting area that has many gifts and wines for sale. This winery was formally Clos Du Muriel. It produces 5,000 cases of wine a year and focuses on Rhône varieties.

Their literature states that they've made a name for themselves for their ultra-premium, handcrafted wines. Perhaps that refers to their 2001 Cinsault Rosé, Grand Reserve, which won a gold medal at one of the Riverside International Wine Competitions, and a double gold medal and best of class at one of the San Diego International Wine Competitions.

The winery hosts special events including Cinema Classics (the first Saturday of every month), Flamenco Fridays (every Friday evening with music and tapas) and wine tasting classes.

LOCATION: 33410 Rancho California Road, Temecula, California 92591
(909) 506-5500

 WEBSITE: www.miramontewinery.com

 HOURS: 10 a.m. to 4:45 p.m. daily.

 TOURS: Not available.

 TASTING CHARGE: $7 for five samples (includes take-home glass).

 WINES AVAILABLE

White/Blush	Red	DESSERT
Chardonnay	Old Vine Zinfandel	Opulente Meritage
Riesling	Red Rhapsody	
Rosé Cinsault	Syrah	
Sangiovese Rosé		
Sauvignon Blanc		
Viognier		
White Rhapsody		

 DIRECTIONS: Take I-15 to the Rancho California Road exit. Miramonte Winery is on the left side of the road as you head east and is located past the Loma Vista Bed and Breakfast.

Mount Palomar Winery

Mount Palomar Winery seems to be making a name for the Temecula Valley. It has won a number of awards for its wines such as the Best of Show award at the February 1999 Monterey Wine Competition. Their Cortese and Viognier are gold medal winners.

The first vines were planted in 1969; the winery opened in 1975. The founder was John Poole. Currently his son Peter directs the winery. Mount Palomar is one of the Temecula Valley's leaders in testing new grape varieties in the region.

Most of the time the winery draws huge crowds, so be prepared for lots of company. There is a gift shop that sells everything from wine, cheese, and bread to plates, picnic baskets, corks, and wall hangings.

There is a deli with a wide selection of food items. A picnic area and group catering are also available.

While I was taking a tour, our tour director spoke in smooth, slow harmonizing tones that had a hint of a French accent. She had spent six years in France studying wine. She spoke of the wine process and how grapes are hand-picked at midnight to avoid the heat. Inside the cellar we saw oak barrels from France (America's oak barrels don't produce the same taste in wine). Each barrel costs about $600 and is good for about 5 years.

LOCATION: 33820 Rancho California Road, Temecula, California 92591
(909) 676-5047

 WEBSITE: www.mountpalomar.com

 HOURS: 10 a.m. to 5 p.m. daily.

 TOURS: For groups of fifteen or more.

 TASTING CHARGE: $5 to taste six wines (includes take-home glass).

 WINES AVAILABLE
Their Castelleto 1993 "Temecula" Sangiovese is popular.

White	Red	Dessert
Chardonnay	Carignane	Cream Sherry
Cortese	Merlot	Port
	Sangiovese	
	Syrah	
	Shorty's Bistro	
	(Barbera-Sangiovese)	
	Trivato/Super Tuscan	

 DIRECTIONS: From I-15 exit at Rancho California Road and drive east. The winery is about 5 miles down the road and on the left.

Palumbo Family Vineyards & Winery

One of the newest wineries in the area, The Palumbo Family Vineyards would be hard to miss if it weren't for the wine barrel out front with a sign saying "winery" pointing to the driveway. The wine tasting attendant mentioned that the family purchased the home prior to opening the winery in order to make the process of opening a winery easier. Since they're near residences, they had to get permission from the neighbors to open the tasting room. When I asked the attendant if they had tours, he walked me behind the tasting room to show me the barrels and wine that was out in the open fermenting. This is a small winery, where you'll get individual attention. The winery also understands the value of quality wine and has decided to focus on red (mostly French variety) wines. They are dedicated to growing small-lot, handcrafted wines and have 12 acres surrounding the tasting room. If you like intimate gatherings, they offer small wine lunches that include tastings and discussions about their wines.

LOCATION: 40150 Barksdale Circle, Temecula, California 92591
(909) 676-7900

 WEBSITE: www.palumbofamilyvineyards.com

 HOURS: Friday, 12 to 5 p.m., Saturday, 10 a.m to 5 p.m.

 TOURS: No set tours; ask for a tour of their back room!

 TASTING CHARGE: $3.

 WINES AVAILABLE:
Red
Cabernet Franc
Late Harvest Merlot
Sangiovese
Tre Fratelli

 DIRECTIONS: Take Rancho California Road east to Monte de Oro Road. Make a right. Make another right at Barksdale Circle. Look for the wine barrel directing you.

Ponte Family Estate

This new winery on Rancho California Road is built to resemble a farmhouse (but a better word to describe it would be "farmhouse chic"), with vineyards out front and a large gift room full of rooster and wine memorabilia, and a large tasting area. The winery also has a much-needed restaurant called the "Smokehouse Cafe." Much needed, because this growing region does not have a lot of options for dining. The cafe focuses on the local farmers' markets for inspiration and offers dining on their veranda.

The tasting room is surrounded by 350 acres of vineyards. Look for special events such as cooking classes and wine and cigar receptions.

A unique feature of this winery is the restored chapel cellar and barrel room. Its stone front is reminiscent of buildings seen in Europe, and the stones look as though they could've come from the ground nearby.

LOCATION: 35053 Rancho California Road, Temecula California 92591
(909) 694-8855

 WEBSITE: www.pontewinery.com

 HOURS: Daily 10 a.m. to 5 p.m.

 TOURS: Not Available.

 TASTING CHARGE: $6 for logo glass and five tastings.

 **WINES AVAILABLE:**

White	Red
Chardonnay	Barbera
Chenin Blanc	Cabernet
Sauvignon Blanc	Merlot
	Nebbiolo
	Sangiovese
	Zinfandel

 DIRECTIONS: Take I-15 to the Rancho California Road exit. The winery is located on the right, heading east, after South Coast Winery.

Santa Margarita Winery

   Driving to Santa Margarita Winery, one of the original Temecula wineries that came after Calloway and Mount Palomar, is a bit rough because of the bumpy dirt road on which it is located. The winery's main product is Cabernet Sauvignon. Their first crush was in 1985 and according to the owner, they sell out of their product each year. They produce less than 1,000 cases of wine each year.

   You will have to be tenacious to find this winery. Sometimes it closes when they run out of wine; call before you visit.

LOCATION: 33490 Madera de Playa, Temecula, California 92592
(909) 676-4431

 WEBSITE: Not available.

 HOURS: 11 a.m. to 4 p.m. weekends, November to early spring. The winery posts a "closed" sign when it is out of wine.

 TOURS: Not available.

 TASTING CHARGE: Complimentary.

 WINES AVAILABLE
Red
Cabernet Sauvignon

 DIRECTIONS: Take I-15 to Rancho California Road exit. Head east on Rancho California Road to Calle Contento. Make a right. Then turn right on Madera de Playa, a dirt road.

South Coast Winery & Temecula Springs Resort

This winery has the distinction of having the grandest scheme in the Temecula Valley. When I was there, the spa and bungalows were in the building phase, but the structure is there and I'm counting the days before I can try one of their spa treatments and stay in one of the bungalows. The corner lot location has a panoramic view of the mountains surrounding the area and a rustic wood trellis lines the path to the tasting room from the parking area. Here's what they'll have once all the building is done: A restaurant called the Vineyard Rosé (featuring California-style cuisine), The GrapeSeed Spa (including a full-service beauty salon, swimming pool, fitness room, yoga/aerobics, and a spa boutique). You'll be able to choose from a number of spa treatments including massages, facials, and manicures. The gift shop will offer unique items as well as food products for gift baskets and picnics. There will be a 70,000 square foot indoor and outdoor meeting space including various conference rooms. The accommodations will include 76 bungalow suites in what they're terming "California Style" decor. The suites will have special touches like Jacuzzi tubs, plush robes, fireside sitting area, and a complimentary daily newspaper.

The winery uses grapes from their own vineyard in a valley near Palomar Mountain, and also purchases grapes grown in Temecula and other areas of the South Coast regions for their wines.

LOCATION: 34843 Rancho California Road, Temecula California 92591
(909) 587-9463

 WEBSITE: www.wine-resort.com

 HOURS: 10 a.m to 5 p.m. weekends.

 TOURS: Not available.

 TASTING CHARGE: $5 to taste six wines (includes a take-home glass).

 WINES AVAILABLE:

White	**Red**
Cabernet Rose	Sangiovese
Chardonnay	Zinfandel
Sauvignon Blanc	
Viognier	

 DIRECTIONS: Take I-15 toward Temecula. Take the Rancho California Road exit. Head east. Located on the right side after Van Roekel Vineyards & Winery.

Stuart Cellars Winery

Stuart Cellars is a newer winery in the Temecula Valley that started in 1998. That year, the winery produced 6,000 cases of wine. The residence in front doesn't reveal the treasure inside the tasting room. You'll find an Old World experience here unlike the other tasting rooms in the Valley. You'll walk on gorgeous tile; rich tapestries line the walls of the room. The tasting room is painted with warm, friendly colors. Their vineyard is planted in the French tradition which allows grapes to age evenly on each side of the vine and offers more fruit consistency. It also helps to protect the grapes from the hot summer sun by providing a canopy.

Their red Meritage blend, Tabria, won a silver medal at one of the Jerry Mead Wine Competitions.

There are picnic tables outside and a 360-degree view of the surrounding area. Gifts are for sale inside the tasting room.

LOCATION: 33515 Rancho California Road, Temecula, California 92591
(909) 676-6414 or (888) 260-0870

 WEBSITE: www.stuartcellars.com

 HOURS: 10 a.m. to 5 p.m. daily.

 TOURS: Arranged for large groups.

 TASTING CHARGE: $8 allows you a taste of five wines (includes a take-home glass).

 WINES AVAILABLE

White	Red	Dessert
Callista	Cabernet Sauvignon	Muscat
Chardonnay	Sangiovese	Port
Viognier	Zinfandel	
	Tabia (Meritage)	

 DIRECTIONS: Take I-15 to the Rancho California Road exit. Head east. Stuart Cellars Winery is located just past Thornton Winery on the right side of the road.

Thornton Winery

Thornton Winery, which opened in 1988 and was originally called Culbertson, is a popular place for wedding receptions because of its large estate-like building and grounds. This winery can probably take the prize for having the most European-inspired look in the Valley.

As you walk through the entrance to the winery, you'll find a manicured herb garden that the winery's restaurant chefs use to prepare meals.

An air-conditioned gift shop has one of the most extensive collections of gifts in the Valley. Through a large window in the gift shop you can watch people tasting wine. Everything inside the gift shop is immaculate.

The winery has a champagne tasting bar and a restaurant, The Café Champagne. The winery also hosts a Champagne Jazz series on Sundays with live music. There are areas for banquets and weddings.

Their Cuvee Rouge sparkling wine won a gold medal at one of the West Coast Wine Competitions.

Thornton's wines are easily found at area wine shops and stores, but it's hard not to stop by this impressive winery. Learn about their "méthode champenoise" process while you're there. They use it for their sparkling wine production.

LOCATION: 32575 Rancho California Road, Temecula, California 92591
(909) 699-0099

 WEBSITE: www.thorntonwine.com

 HOURS: 10 a.m. to 5 p.m. daily.

 TOURS: Weekend tours only.

 TASTING CHARGE: Varies (charged by the glass or for groups of tastes).

 WINES AVAILABLE
Thornton Winery is known for its champagne (the winery has a 1990 Brut Reserve). They also produce red wines and are known for their sparkling wines.

White	Red	Dessert
Chardonnay	Barbera	Aleatico
Pinot Blanc	Cabernet-Merlot	
Viognier	Carignane	
	Côte Red (Rhône blend)	
	Syrah	
	Zinfandel	

 DIRECTIONS: Take I-15 and exit at Rancho California Road. The winery is located 4 miles east. It is the first winery on the right.

Van Roekel Vineyard & Winery

Van Roekel Vineyard & Winery was built in 1982. It first began operating as Mesa Verde Vineyards. Currently it is owned by the Van Roekels who also operate Maurice Carrie Winery.

This growing winery is marked by several red buildings with Spanish-tiled roofs. The winery stands out for its red, barn-like appearance. There are deli foods for sale, a gift shop, a picnic area, and a playground.

Van Roekel has won gold medals for their Gerwurtztraminers at one of the Jerry Mead Wine Competitions, and their Muscat of Alexandria dessert wine won a gold at one of the Pacific Rim Competitions.

LOCATION: 34567 Rancho California Road, Temecula, California 92591
(909) 699-6961

 WEBSITE: www.mauricecarriewinery.com

 HOURS: 10 a.m. to 5 p.m. daily.

 TOURS: Not available.

 TASTING CHARGE: $5 to taste five wines (includes a take-home glass).

 WINES AVAILABLE

White/Blush	Red	Dessert
Blush-Rosé	Cabernet Sauvignon	Red dessert wine
Cabernet Franc	Grenache	
Chardonnay	Merlot	
Fumé Blanc	Petit Syrah	
Gerwürtztraminer	Zinfandel	
Pinot Blanc		
Rosé of Syrah		

 DIRECTIONS: Take I-15 to the Rancho California Road exit. Head east on Rancho California Road. The winery is located on the right, approximately 7 miles from the freeway.

Wilson Creek

Wilson Creek Winery is known around town as the winery that has the almond champagne–or more technically, sparkling wine. While I was there, limos lined the parking lot and the staff was busy tending to a wedding. Two wine tasting areas were open, one in the front room surrounded by gifts, the other in the back with the wine barrels and make-shift tables to handle the eager tasting crowd.

Wilson Creek is a family-owned winery. A number of family members live on-site. They bought the 20-acre property, according to their website, in 1996 and built the winery in 1998. Currently, they produce about 15,000 cases of wine.

A white gazebo sits on the front lawn surrounded by roses and flowers, and a creek where you can occasionally spot ducks and frogs.

LOCATION: 35960 Rancho California Road, Temecula, California 92591
(909) 699-9463

 WEBSITE: www.wilsoncreekwinery.com

 HOURS: 10 a.m. to 5 p.m. daily.

 TOURS: Special arrangement for groups.

 TASTING CHARGE: $6 (includes a take-home glass).

 WINES AVAILABLE:

White/Blush	Red
Almond Sparkling wine	Cabernet Sauvignon
Chardonnay	Merlot
White Cabernet Sauvignon	Zinfandel

 DIRECTIONS: Take I-15 to the Rancho California Road exit. Head east on Rancho California Road. The winery is located on the left, the furthest winery to the east.

Wineries of Baja California

Although Baja's wineries are about a two-hour drive from San Diego (on a good day), information is being included here on these wineries because of San Diegans' frequent trips across the border. Also, this winery area is really burgeoning.

Wineries in Mexico are a fun excursion when you're already planning a trip south of the border. Almost all of Mexico's wines are produced in Ensenada and the Guadalupe Valley.

There are four wineries that you can visit in Baja California that do not require advance reservations. They are L.A. Cetto in Tijuana, Casa Pedro Domecq, Bodegas de Santo Tomás Winery, and Vina de Liceaga.

My companion and I spent a weekend in Bajamar, between Rosarito and Ensenada, and then took a drive down Highway 1 to look for the wineries near the Santo Tomás area. Although we spoke with a number of people at the hotel, only a visitor could tell us how to get to the wineries and then when we drove there, we saw no signs welcoming visitors. We think we found some vineyards and a building that could have been a winery, but it was hard to tell. We later found out that the Santo Tomás area is where vineyards are but not wine tasting. I recommend taking a tour to Mexico at first so that the itinerary is set up for you when you arrive. Try calling Baja California Tours, mentioned later in this chapter, to arrange a trip.

The burgeoning Guadalupe Valley area has plans to create what the wineries are calling a "Grape Corridor," which would include improving the roads, and adding more signs to direct people to the wineries. There are 13 vintners in the area, but not all of them are opening their doors to the public right now. That might change as the government realizes the tourism potential of this region.

One of the inns that may be taking advantage of this new interest in the area is the **Adobe Guadalupe Inn**, located in the heart of the Guadalupe Valley. Call the six-room inn for reservations, 011-52-64615-52-094 or (949) 631-30987, or see their website: www.adobeguadalupe.com. The inn is a working winery with 60 acres of vines. They have six guest rooms, and a large Mexican breakfast is served in the morning.

Fee

There is a tourist fee in effect throughout Mexico. However, short-term visitors to Baja California's main tourist areas do not have to pay the fee, which applies to tourists who remain in Mexico for longer than 72 hours.

Cash

It should be noted that most of the wineries accept only cash. Some restaurants and hotels will take credit cards, but it's better to carry cash just in case. There is no need to change your dollars into pesos, as the dollar is accepted throughout the tourist region. However, if you will be traveling beyond the border areas, you may want to convert some of your dollars into pesos.

Don't Drink the Water

Remember to avoid tap water while you're in Mexico. It's a good idea to bring bottled water with you or to purchase bottled water there. It is safe to drink the beer, soda, and wine available. However, you may want to avoid dairy products and fruits and vegetables.

"No Comprendo"

Most of the Mexican people working in the border areas know some English. Therefore, if no one in your party speaks Spanish, you should still be able to get by in these areas. Just in case you run into someone who doesn't speak English, you may want to bring a Spanish dictionary with you.

Insurance

If you are driving into Mexico, you should insure your car with Mexican insurance. Unfortunately, only Mexican-licensed insurance companies are recognized in Mexico.

Did you know that during Prohibition, many Americans traveled to Mexico to buy liquor?

Tour Companies

Baja California Tours, Inc.
7734 Herschel Avenue, Suite O, La Jolla, California 92037
(858) 454-7166

Hours: 8:30 a.m. to 5 p.m. weekdays.

Baja California Tours offers tours to the Mexican wine country. One tour called "Wine & Dine in Ensenada" goes to Casa Pedro Domecq Winery, L.A. Cetto Winery, and Château Camou. The tour also includes lunch at L.A. Cetto Winery. Call the tour company for rates and schedules. Groups may be able to reserve a date of their own.

The "Wine & Dine in Ensenada" bus tour begins at the Kings Inn in Mission Valley. When we took the tour, a bus picked us up at Kings Inn and we headed to Mexico a little after 9 a.m.

We had two tour directors. One was a young woman who lives in the Tijuana area and is taking journalism courses there. She taught us about the Mexican culture. It was very informative and gave us insight into the people of the area. The other tour director was a wine expert who works at Vintage Wines. He has been working at the shop for 13 years and knows a lot about wines.

This is a good way to test out the wineries in Mexico, especially if you are unfamiliar with the area.

Lodging

If you're already in Mexico, you can stop by Villa Marina Hotel (located at avenidas Lopez Mateos and Blancarte in Ensenada) to find out about scheduled winery tours. Ask at the front desk.

Adobe Guadalupe Inn
Located in the Guadalupe Valley near the wineries.
01152 (646) 155-2094
(949) 733-2744

Las Rosas Hotel
Highway 1 north of Ensenada. Call for room rates.
01152 (646) 174-4360

Bajamar-Golf Resort
Highway 1 south of Ensenada. Call for room rates.
(888) 311-6076

Las Rocas
Located in Rosarito. Call for room rates.
(888) 527-7622

Ensenada Tourism Office
01152 (617) 723-000 or 723-022
www.bajaquest.com

You can go to the State Tourism Office between avenidas Lopez Mateos and Espinoza or to the tourist information booth at Boulevard Lazaro Cardenas (Boulevard Costero).

Telephoning Mexico
If you need to call one of the Mexican locations listed in this book from the United States, start with the numbers 01152. Then add the area code and the number.

Wineries without Tasting Rooms

Bodegas San Antônio in the San Antônio de las Minas area does not currently have a tasting room.

Call 01152 (646) 174-0078 for more information.

Casa de Piedra, located on Highway 3 at Km 93.5
01152 (615) 5-3097

Also, Mogor-Badán is a winery in Ensenada but it has no tasting facility. Call 01152 (646) 177-1484 for more information.

California allows each adult over the age of 21 to bring back one bottle of wine each month from Mexico.

Ensenada

Please note that directions to the wineries are in relation to the toll road, Mex 1-D. There is also a free road that is named Mex 1.

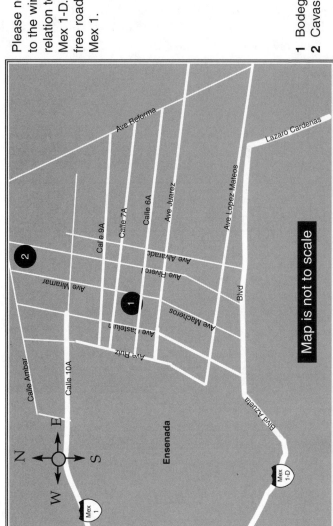

Map is not to scale

1 Bodegas de Santo Tomás
2 Cavas Valmar

Ensenada

Juan Rodriguez Cabrillo first discovered Ensenada many years ago. Then Ensenada was named 60 years later by the explorer Sebastián Vizcaino. However, the region was not settled for many years after that because there was no fresh water in the area. Even today, the areas of Rosarito and Ensenada have limited supplies of fresh water; therefore, their main source of income is through tourists who visit the beaches and shops.

In 1697, the Spanish padres settled in the Baja California area and founded missions. Before that time, wandering Indians occupied the land. In the 1700s, the mission fathers began teaching the Indians how to grow grapes and press wine. The wine was then exchanged for other goods.

Bodegas de Santo Tomás Winery

Although this is Mexico's second-oldest winery, it was actually the first winery in Mexico to produce wines for commercial use. Now the winery, which started in 1888, is venturing into another first. It is partnering with a winery in Northern California, Wente Vineyards, to produce a Cabernet Sauvignon that will be sold in both Mexico and the United States. The wine will be produced at the Bodegas de Santo Tomás winery in Ensenada.

Hugo d'Acosta is the winemaker and he values quality over quantity. He proved his value when he became the winemaker in 1988 and reduced the number of cases made at the winery each year from 200,000 to 80,000. He was trained in Italy.

The building is draped in ivy and stands out from the other buildings surrounding it. Across the street from the winery you'll find a gourmet market and restaurants. When we were there, classical music was playing at a restaurant where people relaxed at outside tables.

LOCATION: Avenida Miramar at Calle #666, downtown Ensenada, Baja California, Mexico 22800
A location in the Santo Tomás area is being built.
01152 (646) 178-3433

WEBSITE: www.santotomas.com.mx

HOURS: The winery opens only during the tour hours (make sure you're on time).

TOURS: Daily 10 a.m., 11 a.m., 12 p.m., 1 p.m., and 3 p.m.

TASTING CHARGE: $2 (includes tour and tasting).

WINES AVAILABLE

White	Red
Chardonnay	Barbera
Chenin Blanc	Cabernet Sauvignon
	Merlot
	Tempranillo

DIRECTIONS: From Tijuana, take Highway 1-D (toll road) toward Ensenada. The winery is located about 60 miles south of Tijuana. As you arrive in Ensenada, the toll road turns into Blvd Azueta. Blvd Azueta turns into Ave Castelum. Head north to Calle 6A. Make a right at Calle 6A and a left at Miramar Ave. The winery is between Calle 6A and 7A in Ensenada. It is located about a 1/2 mile from the main tourist area of Lopez Mateos. It's an easy walk from there. As you're heading north on Miramar Ave., the winery will be on the right.

Cavas Valmar Winery

The vineyards of Cavas Valmar Winery are located in the Guadalupe and San Vicente valleys. The winery opened in 1983, but did not become commercial until 1985.

The winemaker is Fernando Martain. He and his wife, Yolanda, started making wine in their garage and later built the winery that stands today. The winery is located in front of a vineyard planted by Yolanda's grandfather. It is one of the smallest wineries in Mexico. The winery ages the Chenin Blanc wines in stainless steel and the Cabernet Sauvignon in French oak barrels, and is committed to making quality wines.

This building stands out for its red color and the trees and shrubs that surround it.

LOCATION: The winery is located on the corner of Riverol Avenue and Ambar in Ensenada.

Riveroll #1950, Ensenada, Mexico

01152 (646) 178 6405 or 178-2509

 WEBSITE: www.cavasvalmar.com (in Spanish)

 HOURS: By appointment only.

 TOURS: By appointment only.

 TASTING CHARGE: Check with winery.

 WINE AVAILABLE

White	Red
Chardonnay	Cabernet Sauvignon
Chenin Blanc	Tempranillo

 DIRECTIONS: From Tijuana take Highway 1-D (toll road) toward Ensenada. As you arrive in Ensenada the toll road turns into Blvd Azueta. Blvd Azueta turns into Ave Castelum. Take that to Ave Juarez and make a right. Make a left at Ave Riveroll and take the avenue north until it ends at Calle Ambar. The winery is located on the right and has a dirt parking area.

Santo Tomás

Located about 30 miles south of Ensenada, this area is known in Mexico for its wines–but don't look for tasting wine here. A lot of the wine is actually made in Ensenada and not all of the grapes are from Santo Tomás. Go to either the Guadalupe Valley or Ensenada to taste wines. The area is located in a valley surrounded by steep mountains 15 miles from the ocean. Originally, the valley was planted with vineyards but unfortunately there wasn't enough water available to irrigate the land and now only the lower portion of the vineyards still thrive.

The region is a long-time agricultural community that once had a mission. Originally there were 1,000 Indians there who raised sheep and cattle. A Dominican, Padre Loriente, founded the original mission in 1791. It was a Jesuit priest by the name of Juan de Ugarte who planted European grape vines there.

Dominicans originally grew grapes so that they could produce altar wines. For a while, the mission was prosperous but unfortunately an epidemic wiped out the Indians.

Guadalupe Valley

The Guadalupe Valley in Baja California is a wine region that is transitioning, growing, and beginning to produce fine wines. Most of the area has vineyards that are many years old but have been neglected. Only now have people in the area begun to tend to these vines.

Most of the wines produced in Mexico are not consumed by Mexicans. They are exported. However, some of these wines aren't available in the United States. Recently, though it seems Baja Californians have discovered wine tasting as wine bars are becoming more abundant in Ensenada.

The key to this region, and to fine wines, is the climate. It is warm in the inland valley during the day, but cool ocean air brings the temperature down at night. The area's climate can be compared to that of the Mediterranean.

The first vineyards were planted in 1521 by Spanish landowners. It has been said that all landowners in Mexico had to plant vines in order for Mexico to become self-sufficient in the wine business. In the early 1900s, the Guadalupe Valley was settled by Russian immigrants. The Russians developed the Guadalupe Valley into an agricultural community and planted wheat in the fields; later, grape vines were planted for winemaking. The grapes were taken into Tijuana and made into wine.

Did you know that most of the grapes planted in Mexico actually have a different root stalk than the variety that is grown for its wine grapes? Usually a European vine is grafted on top of the root stalk. It takes from 3 to 4 years to get the first crop after planting, and 7 to 8 years to produce crops of good quality.

Today, however (besides a small museum containing Russian artifacts), there is little trace of the Russian heritage. In those days, people would acquire land by working the soil, but would eventually abandon it due to lack of water and other resources. Therefore, many vineyards were not taken care of. The area has a microclimate for grapes and a long, cool growing season.

Fiesta de la Vendimia

The Fiesta de la Vendimia is an annual festival that began in the early 1990s and is usually held in August or September. The festival is put on by the L.A. Cetto Winery; the location of the event changes from year to year. It was established to celebrate the harvest, and attractions usually include grape stomping, live music, and food and wine tasting.

Baja California Tours usually runs a tour for the festival (or you can drive there yourself). Purchase tickets in advance by calling the winery at 01152 (668) 5-3031.

DIRECTIONS: To get to the Guadalupe Valley, take I-5 south from San Diego to the border. Once you are in Mexico, take Highway 1-D. This is a toll road. There are three toll stops to Ensenada. When you get to Highway Mexico 3 headed to Tecate at El Sauzal, you are on your way to the Guadalupe Valley. It's about 70 miles from the border to the wineries. Signs will direct you.

Did you know that Mexicans' first choice in liquor is actually brandy? It's their No. 1 alcoholic beverage choice according to our Baja California tour guide.

Guadalupe Valley

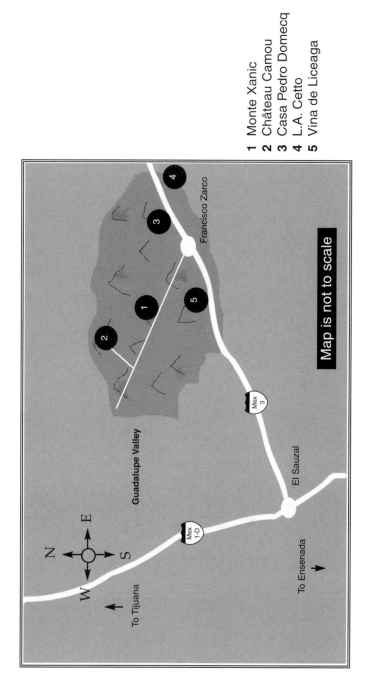

1 Monte Xanic
2 Château Camou
3 Casa Pedro Domecq
4 L.A. Cetto
5 Vina de Liceaga

Map is not to scale

Guadalupe Valley

Francisco Zarco

Mex 3

El Sauzal

Mex 1-D

To Tijuana

To Ensenada

N E S W

Casa Pedro Domecq

This winery, which began in 1972, exports its wine all over the world. Some of the wines it produces are Cabernet Sauvignon, Merlot, Sémillion, and Nebbiolo. There is a large tasting room at the winery, which has an immense collection of Yugoslavian barrels that they age some of their wines in. In the 1600s wines were stored in vases; the winery still has these antiques on display. The winery also stores wines in American oak barrels. The barrels are kept in long, dark caves that have dim orange lighting. The dim lighting is to protect the color of the wine in the bottles. As you walk through the cave, you'll find an area that houses a replica of the Virgin of Guadalupe. It looks like a shrine. The caves have a total capacity of 32,000 bottles of wine. The winemaker is Ron McClendon, who emphasizes quality in Domecq's wine.

LOCATION: Guadalupe Valley
Valle de Guadalupe, Highway 3, km 73
01152 (646) 155 2254
Ensenada "Domecq's Fine Wine Boutique"
149 Avenida Ruiz, Ensenada
01152 (617) 8-3725

WEBSITE: www.domecq.com.mx (in Spanish)

HOURS: Guadalupe Valley 9 a.m. to 4:30 p.m. weekdays, and 9 a.m. to 1 p.m. Saturday.

TOURS: Guadalupe Valley Call to arrange.

TASTING CHARGE: Guadalupe Valley Check with the winery.

HOURS: Ensenada 10 a.m. to 8 p.m. Monday through Saturday; 11 a.m. to 6 p.m. Sunday.

TOURS/TASTING CHARGE: Ensenada Wine tastings are by appointment

WINES AVAILABLE

White	Red
Blanc de Blanc's	Cabernet Sauvignon
Calafia	Calafia
Chateau Domecq	Chateau Domecq
Los Reyes	Los Reyes
Reserva Real	Merlot
Semillion	Nebbiolo
	Reserva Real

DIRECTIONS: Guadalupe - From the border take Highway 1-D south and then Highway Mexico 3 toward Tecate. The winery is located on Highway 3 about 80 miles from the border. **Ensenada** - From Highway 1-D in Ensenada the highway will turn into Blvd Azueta. Make a left on Ave Lopez Mateos and a right on Ave Ruiz.

Château Camou

Château Camou was voted the "Best Baja California Winery" by *San Diego Reader's Best of 2000*. The winery is serious about its wines and has received national media attention as well as awards. Some of the winery equipment has been imported from Beaune France, Italy, Spain and the United States so they're making a considerable investment. These wines are available in the United States (many of the wines produced in Mexico are not). Château Camou's focus is on quality. Its vineyards are planted close together, after the French model of planting. There are between 2,000 and 2,500 vines planted per acre. That means less, but better quality, fruit per vine. This winery is considered a boutique winery and is smaller than others in the valley, but it has a lot of potential. Their inspiration is Bordeaux wines; they're considering taking out their Chardonnay vines and replacing them with Bordeaux. Their front door area is a replica of an old mission and is also represented on their label. The winemaker is Dr. Victor M. Torres Alegre; Michol Rolland has been consulting with the winemaker since 1995.

The winery's vineyards are very old (they have been producing since the 1930s), but the winery is new.

In 1985 Ernest Camou took over the property. Then in 1994 Fernando Favela acquired 50 percent of the property and established the winery. The first vintage for Château Camou was in 1995.

LOCATION: Office: Aldama No. 599-2A, Col. Obrera, Ensenada 22830
Local number 01152 (646) 177 2221

 WEBSITE: www.chateau-camou.com.mx

HOURS: Monday through Saturday from 8 a.m. to 3 p.m., Sunday 9 a.m. to 2 p.m.

TOURS: The winery has various 30-minute tours plus tasting packages to choose from. Cost depends on the package chosen.

TASTING CHARGE: Depends on the package.

WINES AVAILABLE

White	Red
Blanc de Blanc's	Cabernet-Merlot
Chardonnay	Cabernet-Zinfandel
Fumé Blanc	Claret
	Granvino Tinto
	Zinfandel

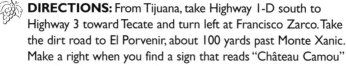 **DIRECTIONS:** From Tijuana, take Highway 1-D south to Highway 3 toward Tecate and turn left at Francisco Zarco. Take the dirt road to El Porvenir, about 100 yards past Monte Xanic. Make a right when you find a sign that reads "Château Camou" and "Canada del Trigo." After about a half mile, take the detour that heads to the right. This will take you to Château Camou. You should be able to see the winery from Francisco Zarco (a dirt road).

L.A. Cetto

L.A. Cetto's founder, Don Angelo Cetto, settled in Baja California in 1926. He was originally from Italy and had a background in winemaking and gained recognition for his wines. The winery in the Guadalupe Valley began in 1975 and in 1979, production of varietal wines began. This is where most of the winemaking takes place. The "L.A. Cetto" name is fairly recent. It began in 1983 after previously being named "Vinicola L.A. Cetto," and before that "Productos de Uva, S.A. de C.V."

The winery has been managed by a long line of Cettos. After Don Angelo founded the winery, his son, Luis Agustin, began running it. Currently Luis Agustin's son, Luis Alberto, operates the winery.

This winery handles all of its own production, and produces brandy as well as wine and olive oil. Currently all bottling is done in Tijuana, where a tasting room and tours are also available. Some of its wine is aged in oak barrels.

This winery has a vast wine cellar and wine tasting boutique in Tijuana. A shuttle bus from Avenue Revoluciòn goes to the winery every 30 minutes. There is no cost for this service. Their wines are internationally acclaimed. The winery holds a yearly L.A. Cetto Harvest Festival in late summer.

LOCATION: (Tijuana and Guadalupe Valley)
Guadalupe Location: Valle de Guadalupe, Highway 3, km 73
01152 (646) 155-2179
Tijuana Tasting Location:
Avenida Cañón Johnson #2108 in Tijuana near Avenue
Constitución and Calle 10
01152 (668) 53031

WEBSITE: www.lacetto.com.mx (in Spanish)

HOURS: Tijuana Location 10 a.m. to 5:30 p.m. Monday
through Saturday.

TOURS: Tijuana Location Every 30 minutes.

TASTING CHARGE: Tijuana Location $2 (without a
take-home glass), $3 (with a take-home glass).

HOURS: Guadalupe Location Call beforehand.

WINES AVAILABLE
The winery's Nebbiolo wine is considered one of their best
(according to our Baja California tour guide).

White	Red
Blanc de Colombard	Cabernet Sauvignon
Chardonnay	Melot
Chenin Blanc	Nebbiolo
Fumé Blanc	Petite Sirah

DIRECTIONS: Guadalupe Location - From Tijuana take
Highway 1 toward Ensenada. Then take Highway Mexico 3
headed to Tecate at El Sauzal. The winery is at kilometer 28 on
Highway 3.
Tijuana Location - From the border head toward Tijuana.
You will end up on Calle 3A (Carrillo Puerto). Turn left at Calle
8A (Hidalgo) and right at Ave Constitution. Cañón Johnson
veers to the right. The winery is on the left.

Monte Xanic

The winery's name stems from "Xanic," which means "the flower that blooms after the first rainfall"; the word comes from the Cora Indians, who live nearby.

Five businessmen got together in 1985 and dreamed of a winery that sold prestigious wines. Tomas Fernàndez wanted to get out of the smog and stress of Mexico City and Dr. Hans Backhoff, who produced wine with other local home winemakers, had been thinking about starting a wine business. Both of them had a lot of interest in fine wines; they met on a boat while they were competing in the Newport-Ensenada Regatta. Their purpose was to make the best wine possible in the region. Their efforts have paid off. The wines are often sold out and they have won numerous awards in various international wine competitions.

In order to maintain quality, the winery workers handpick the grapes at their exact ripeness, and use French barrels to age the wine.

They focus on Bordeaux varietals–Cabernet Sauvignon, Merlot, Sauvignon Blanc, and Sémillon. They also produce Chenin Blanc and Chardonnay. The Chardonnay is aged in new French oak barrels and the Chenin Blanc is aged on lees (grape and yeast residue left in wine after fermentation) in stainless steel tanks. Dr. Backhoff is the winemaker.

If you'd like to order Monte Xanic wine, contact Chalone Wine Group at (707) 254-4200.

LOCATION: Camino El Porvenir, Valle de Guadalupe, Mexico 01152 (646) 174 6155

 WEBSITE: www.montexanic.com

 HOURS: 9 a.m. to 4 p.m. weekdays.

 TOURS: By appointment.

 TASTING CHARGE: Call for information.

 WINES AVAILABLE

White	Red
Chardonnay	Cabernet Sauvignon
Chenin Blanc	Merlot
Chenin Colombard	
Sauvignon Blanc/Sémillon	

 DIRECTIONS: From the border go south on Highway 1-D toward Ensenada. Take Highway 3 to Tecate. Turn left at Francisco Zarco (a dirt road). The winery will be on the right, a couple miles from the turnoff.

Vina de Liceaga

In 2002, this winery was named the best winery in Mexico at the San Francisco International Wine Competition. According to the *San Diego Union-Tribune*, this competition is the most prestigious wine judging event in the country. The judges at the competition gave the winery a "Best of Nation" for their Merlot Gran Reserva 1999. Perhaps other proof is in the gold medals they've won recently. They've received gold medals for their Merlot Gran Reserva 1998, Merlot 1999, Merlot Castillo de Las Minas 2000, Merlot 2000, Cabernet Franc 2001, and Castillo de Las Minas 2000.

The winery was started with the purchase of 50 acres in 1982. In 1983 the vineyard was planted with table grapes, and eventually, by the early 90's, the owners decided to plant wine grapes with the first production of wine in '93. Currently they prduce about 3,000 cases of wine a year.

LOCATION: Km 93 Carretera Tecate-Ensenada, San Antonio de las Minas, Ensenada, B.C., Mexico 22766, 011 (52) (646) 155-3091. In the United States mail to P.O. Box 434487, San Ysidro, California 92143

 WEBSITE: www.vinosliceaga.com

 HOURS: 11 a.m. to 4 p.m. weekends.

 TOURS: Call to set up an appointment.

 TASTING CHARGE: Unavailable

 WINES AVAILABLE:
Red
Vino Tinto Merlot
Vino Tinto Cabernet Sauvignon Grenache
Vino Tinto Merlot Gran Reserva

 DIRECTIONS: From the border take Highway 1-D south and then Highway Mexico 3 toward Tecate. The winery is located off of Highway Mexico 3 in the San Antonio de las Minas area.

Wineries of Los Angeles County

It's ironic that the area where some of the first grape vines were planted in California is now mostly concrete and a huge city of skyscrapers, amusement parks, and movie studios. Los Angeles ranks No. 2 after New York in the media world. In the grape world, it's a tiny player, but some pioneers are trying to regain their share of grape vines. You have to search, however, for the returning pioneers. Although **Semler Malibu Estate Vineyards and Saddlerock Vineyards** in Malibu has 55,000 vines and produce three types of wines (Cabernet Sauvignon, Merlot, and Syrah), they do not currently have a tasting room. They plan to build a tasting room, and occasionally they open their doors to the public for events like grape crushing parties. Call the winery for more event information at (818) 889-0008 or check out their website at www.saddlerockvineyards.com. There is one winery in the heart of the city, two others are located in Rancho Cucamonga, which is technically the Inland Empire area, and another winery is in Santa Clarita (not far from Six Flags Magic Mountain).

On your way to the Rancho Cucamonga wineries you might want to stop at **San Antonio's** additional tasting room, located at 2802 S. Miliken Avenue in Ontario (909) 947-3995. The tasting room is close to Galleano Winery.

Near the Agua Dulce Winery, you might want to check out the **Valencia Wine Company,** located at 24300 Town Center Drive #105 (661) 254-9300 or look at their website at www.valenciawinecompany.com. The shop has a wine bar, classes, a "Meet the Winemaker" night, and of course, a shop full of wine. There is also the **Wine Savor** in Valencia at 24268 Valencia Blvd. (661) 288-2980 or www.wine-savor.com. They boast that every wine in their store is under $10. They also have a wine bar where you can try the wines you plan to buy.

Agua Dulce Winery

When I asked the wine attendant if there were other wineries in the area, he jokingly told me that they were all looking to Agua Dulce to see if they could survive. Although other areas of Los Angeles have previously grown grape vines, this area (located northeast of downtown Los Angeles near Six Flags Magic Mountain) is a first. According to the wine attendant the area has perfect conditions for growing grapes, with temperatures that fluctuate about 30 degrees from, morning to night and soil that has a slightly acidic structure. From the crowd that was there on a Saturday afternoon, it appears the winery might be doing something right.

The drive up Sierra Highway takes you through rolling hills, and past a pumpkin patch (while I was there). Grape vines sit prettily next to the barn and ranch-style building. Inside the tasting room the open ceilings reveal piping and a loft area for members of their wine club. These members are allowed to taste the locally made wines. The regular tasters get samples of wines made from grapes grown elsewhere, primarily from the Paso Robles area.

My companion raved about the French cuisine at **Le Chene Restaurant,** located nearby at 12625 Sierra Highway. Occasionally the restaurant holds wine tastings. Call (661) 251-4315 for more details.

LOCATION: 9640 Sierra Highway, Agua Dulce, California 91350
(661) 268-7402

 WEBSITE: www.aguadulcevineyards.com

 HOURS: Open from 10 a.m. to 5:30 p.m daily.

 TOURS: By appointment.

 TASTING CHARGE: $3 to taste five wines (includes take-home glass).

 WINES AVAILABLE:

Whites	Reds/Zinfandel	Dessert
Chardonnay	Merlot	Muscat of
Sauvignon Blanc	Cabernet Sauvignon	Alexandria
	Syrah	Zinfandel Port
	Sangiovese	

 DIRECTIONS: Take the I-5 freeway headed toward Santa Clarita, then take the 14 freeway north to Agua Dulce Canyon Road. Turn left. After about 3 miles, make a left at the continuation of Agua Dulce Canyon Road.

Galleano Winery

My first thought as I drove to Galleano Winery was that it was an unlikely place for one. Sitting among office warehouses and surrounded by dusty freeways, the winery is like a fort staking its ground among the encroaching enemy. Its rustic buildings are a nod to early America; in fact, the 1890s two-story home on the property still houses the Galleano family. As you drive toward the winery you'll notice small patches of open spaces with what look like neglected grape vines. However, after speaking with the wine attendant at the tasting bar, I found out that the grapes from those vines are sought after by wineries all over California because they're considered "old vine" wine grapes. Their average age is 90. They look neglected because the attendant said they "dry farm" the grapes (meaning that they don't add a single drop of water to them other than the normal rainfall). The winery was recently named a historic winery by the National Register of Historic Places and California Register of Historical Resources. It has been making wine since 1933.

There is a park-like atmosphere across from the tasting room with lots of birds singing nearby, donkeys and geese, and picnicking spots. The staff in the tasting room is very friendly. The view looks out onto the grape vines and farming equipment. While I was there a staff member from Hart Winery in Temecula was tasting wine. Apparently the two share grapes with each other. A number of their wines have won gold medals in various competitions including their 2000 Zinfandel Port, the 2001 Pioneer's Legendary Zinfandel, the Nono's Solera Sherry, and the 1997 Zinfandel Port.

LOCATION: 4231 Wineville Road, Mira Loma, California 91752
(909) 685-5376

 WEBSITE: www.galleanowinery.com

 HOURS: October through March: Monday through Saturday, 9 a.m. to 5 p.m., Sunday 10:30 a.m. to 5 p.m. April through September: Monday through Saturday 9 a.m. to 6 p.m., Sunday 10:30 a.m to 5 p.m.

 TOURS: Weekends between 2 and 4 p.m.

 TASTING CHARGE: No charge.

 WINES AVAILABLE

Whites	**Reds**
Almond Champagne	Cabernet Sauvignon
Candlelight White	Chianti
Champagne	Cucamonga Peak Red
Chardonnay Cucamonga Peak White	Heritage Red
	Merlot
Grenache Rose	Port
Johannisberg Riesling	Sherry
Muscat	Zinfandel
White Zinfandel	

 DIRECTIONS: Take I-15 toward Rancho Cucamonga to the Limonite exit. Head east. Make a left at Wineville Road.

Joseph Filippi Winery

Not far from Galleano Winery is Joseph Filippi Winery, set among a backdrop of hilly mountains and a few vineyards. The tasting room is a complete contrast to Galleano's. Whereas Galleano's could be set in a cowboy movie, Fillipi's tasting room might be more likely to appear in the latest *Sex in the City* episode. The room is very large and is well stocked with a wide range of gift items. You'll find the wine tasting bar near the back, and an art gallery on the second floor.

The winery also has a tasting room in Ontario at an old company town called Guasti near the Ontario airport. The area was founded in 1900 and used to be a working winery but now is more of a tourist location with a historic Mission Revival villa completed in 1923 (weddings and parties often take place here). The estate includes della robia reliefs, frescos, a marble statuary, and European furniture. There is a bakery and café on the premises featuring pastries, sandwiches, and a European-style menu.

The winery is family owned and has been in the hands of a long line of Filippi's. They purchased the current Rancho Cucamonga site–a historical landmark claimed to be the oldest winery in California (formerly called Thomas Winery)–in 1965.

LOCATION: Winery - 12467 Base Line Road, Rancho
Cucamonga, California 91739
(909) 899-5755
Ontario Tasting Room - 2803 East Guasti Road, Ontario,
California 91743
(909) 390-6998

 WEBSITE: www.josephfilippiwinery.com

 HOURS: Daily from 10 a.m. to 6 p.m.

 TOURS: 12 p.m. Wednesday through Sunday.

 TASTING CHARGE: $5 to taste five wines.

 WINES AVAILABLE

Whites	**Red**
Blanc Grenache	Cabernet Sauvignon
Chardonnay	Merlot
Gerwurztraminer	Mourvedre
	Petite Syrah
	Rocehlle
	Sangiovese
	Syrah
	Zinfandel

 DIRECTIONS: To the winery: Take I-15 toward Barstow/Las
Vegas. At Base Line Road in Rancho Cucamonga, head west.
The winery is on the left. To the Ontario tasting room: Take
the I-10 freeway (east if you're coming from Los Angeles, west
if you're coming from San Diego). Exit at Archibald Avenue and
head south. Head east on Guasti Drive. The tasting room is on
the left.

San Antonio Winery

Perhaps San Antonio Winery in Los Angeles can best be described as a dichotomy: "A division or the process of dividing into two especially mutually exclusive or contradictory groups," according to *Webster's Ninth New Collegiate Dictionary*.

On the drive from the I-5 freeway headed north toward Glendale, you'll see a side of the building marking the winery. Hanging street signs along the side roads toward the winery hint of a jewel, but it's hard to know what you're getting into until you walk inside the rounded front door. Set amid a deteriorating section of downtown Los Angeles, and a few strands of barb wire on buildings nearby, its ivy-covered walls only hint at what is revealed inside. Once indoors, the atmosphere turns sophisticated, as if you were in a tasting room in Napa or Temecula. You'll find the tasting bar to the left and a large-stocked gift section to the right.

Wine barrels surround the restaurant's dining area. The winery displays their entrees (actual samples of their food) on a table, so you know exactly what you're getting when you order. They have everything from sandwiches to pastas. And although the food looks and tastes like it's from a nice-quality restaurant, the self-service line brought the experience down a notch. When I was there, the winery set a sophisticated mood with live music and the room was packed on a Sunday afternoon.

Some of my previous research has shown that the Los Angeles area had one of the first commercial growers, Joseph Chapman, in the 1820s, and that there were actually vineyards there. San Antonio Winery hints toward this history. You'll find a marker near the entrance citing the winery as a "City of Los Angeles Cultural Historical Landmark." But, instead of vineyards, you'll find mostly concrete surrounding the area.

A man named Santo Cambianica began San Antonio Winery in 1917. His nephew, Stefano Riboli, continued his tradition and today it is still owned by the same family. Although there are no vineyards at the winery, the family owns vineyards in Napa Valley and elsewhere and makes their wine from grapes grown there. This is a place to experience some of the early history of the wine business before it moved elsewhere. You can almost imagine what it would've been like in the early 1900s.

 LOCATION: 737 Lamar Street, Los Angeles, California 90031 (323) 223-1401

 WEBSITE: www.sanantoniowinery.com

 HOURS: Open daily (except major holidays) 10 a.m. to 6 p.m.

 TOURS: Available, call for details.

 TASTING CHARGE: No cost.

 WINES AVAILABLE

Whites	Red	Dessert
Chardonnay	Cabernet Sauvignon	Madeira Port
Pinot Grigio	Pinot Noir	Marsala Sherry
White Zinfandel	Petite Sirah	Muscat Canelli
	Merlot	

 DIRECTIONS: You'll see the signs for the winery off I-5. Head toward Los Angeles on I-5. At North Main Street, near the 110 freeway, head west, then make a left at Lamar.

San Diego
Wine Tasting Events

The following restaurants and stores often hold wine tastings and related events. Please call each location for information as each has different schedules throughout the year.

BERNARD'O RESTAURANT
12457 Rancho Bernardo Road, Rancho Bernardo
(858) 487-7171
Holds wine dinners.

CUVEE
5656 La Jolla Boulevard, La Jolla
(858) 551-4090
Holds wine tastings and wine dinners.

BLUE BAY CAFÉ
3780 Ingrahm Street, Pacific Beach
(858) 581-0200
Holds happy hour wine tastings.

CARVERS
11940 Bernardo Plaza Drive, Rancho Bernardo
(858) 485-1262
Holds wine tastings the first Tuesday of every month.

GEORGE'S AT THE COVE
1250 Prospect Street, La Jolla
(858) 454-4244
Holds winemaker dinners.

LAUREL RESTAURANT
505 Laurel Street, Bankers Hill
(619) 239-2222
Holds wine tastings.

MERITAGE
897 South Coast Highway 101, Suite F-104, Encinitas
(760) 634-3350
Holds "Wine Lover's Nights" offering 50 percent off certain bottles
of wines; happy hour every night.

MORTON'S OF CHICAGO
285 J Street, San Diego
(619) 696-3367
Call for event schedule.

NAPA VALLEY GRILLE
At Horton Plaza next to Nordstrom, Downtown San Diego
(619) 238-5440
Has "Wine Tasting Wednesdays."

SAN DIEGO WINE COMPANY
5282 Eastgate Mall, Miramar
(858) 535-1400
Holds wine tastings on Saturdays.

THEE BUNGALOW RESTAURANT
4996 W. Point Loma Boulevard, Ocean Beach
(619) 224-2884
Holds wine dinners featuring winemakers.

THE HARBOR'S EDGE RESTAURANT
Sheraton San Diego Hotel and Marina
1380 Harbor Island Drive, Downtown
(619) 692-2255
Holds winemakers' dinners.

VINTAGE WINES
6904 Miramar Road, Miramar
(858) 549-2168
Holds wine tastings.

THE WINESELLER & BRASSERIE RESTAURANT
9550 Waples Street, Sorrento Mesa
(858) 450-9557
Holds wine tasting events every Saturday and on the second Sunday of each month.

WINE BANK
363 Fifth Avenue, Suite 100, corner of 5th and J Streets
(619) 234-7487
Holds wine tastings on Wednesday and Saturday.

WINE STREET
6986 El Camino Real, Carlsbad
(760) 431-8455
Holds wine tastings every Friday.

Calendar of Wine-Related Events

The following is a sample of events happening throughout the year.

FEBRUARY
Barrel wine tasting hosted by the Temecula Valley Vintners'
Association. Two-day event includes gourmet foods and wines from
the barrel.
(800) 801-9463 (for tickets and event schedules)

Bellefleur Restaurant & Winery
Holds a class for people interested in growing wine grapes at home.
Call the winery for information.
(760) 603-1919

APRIL–OCTOBER
Jazz and music concerts at various wineries in Temecula.

Temecula Balloon and Wine Festival
(909) 676-6713

MAY
Temecula Spring Passport Tasting hosted by the Temecula Valley
Vintners' Association

JULY
Wine & Jazz by Baily Vineyard & Winery
(909) 676-9463

AUGUST/SEPTEMBER
Fiesta de la Vendimia (Mexico)
Temecula Wine Auction Weekend hosted by the Temecula Valley
Vintners' Association

SEPTEMBER
Julian Fall Apple Harvest
(760) 765-1857

KPBS Wine & Food Festival
(619) 594-1515

OCTOBER
Art & Wine Festival
(858) 487-1767

NOVEMBER
Temecula-Noveau Celebration Release of new wines
(909) 699-3626

San Diego Wine Bars

THE GRAPE

823 Fifth Avenue, San Diego (Gaslamp Quarter)
(619) 238-8010
Hours: Monday through Thursday. 5:00 p.m. to midnight. Friday and
Saturday 5:00 p.m. to 2 a.m. and Sunday 6 p.m. to midnight.

The location of this wine bar is where the crowds are on Fifth
Avenue in the Gaslamp Quarter. Outside you can sit at tables and
watch the people go by and inside there's a thin, long bar with tables
on both sides. The wine tasting atmosphere is achieved by the use of
wine barrels as tables and an ivy-covered entrance. The wine menu is
extensive; appetizers are available. The Grape offers wines by the glass
as well as flights of three tastes of wine, and most are of different
varietals. I tried a flight that included three wine tastes including the
varietals Viognier and Chardonnay that cost $12.

THE WINE LOVER

3968 Fifth Avenue, Hillcrest
(619) 294-9200
Hours: Monday through Saturday 4:30 p.m. to midnight.
Sunday 4:00 p.m. to 10 p.m.

This bar is an ugly duckling-turned-swan story. Formerly a dive bar
that used to feature men clad in leather and chains and not much
else, The Wine Lover now has mood lighting, and is centered around
a curved bar in the middle with tables and chairs on each side. It's
small, so you have to squeeze by the bar and gifts to get to the back
tables, but it's worth it. The bar has a sophisticated tone. The
bartenders are friendly and there is a long list of wines available. We
tried two flights (four samples of one wine variety) that seem to get
fuller the closer you get to the last sample. The flights may sound
expensive at first but considering the cost to sample a flight of a wine

variety is not much more than a per-glass cost, it was worth it. I also know now which I liked best (of course it was the most expensive one!). You might want to order one flight and share it with a friend. It was fun sharing my flight and comparing tasting notes with my companion. When we were there the crowd was manageable but the staff mentioned that it's usually pretty crowded, so you might want to get there early.

GAFFNEY'S WINE BAR
897 South Coast Highway 101, Encinitas
(760) 633-1011
Hours: Call for hours

This wine bar sits in a cute strip mall in Encinitas surrounded by unique stores. The owners opened their first wine bar in Sonoma, and they offer unique dinners, suggested wine pairings, and special events. Call for more details.

Specialty Wine Retailers

BARONS
Provides a large selection of discounted wine.

Del Mar
12875 El Camino Real
(858) 481-2323

Point Loma
4001 West Point Loma Boulevard
(619) 223-4397

Rancho Bernardo
11828 Rancho Bernardo Road
(858) 485-8686

BEVERAGES & MORE
Offers large selection of wine at reduced prices.

Carmel Mountain
11475 Carmel Mountain Road
(858) 673-3892

Encinitas
212 North El Camino Real
(760) 943-6631

La Mesa
8410 Center Drive
(619) 461-6230

Mission Valley
925 Camino de la Reina
(619) 295-3171

COST PLUS
Has a large wine section.

Chula Vista
2464 Mackenzie Creek Road
(619) 397-7944

Downtown San Diego
372 Fourth Avenue
(619) 236-1737

La Jolla
8657 Villa La Jolla Drive
(858) 455-8210

La Mesa
5500 Grossmont Center Drive
(619) 466-2991

HOLIDAY WINE CELLAR
This shop has an actual wine cellar and sells rare and vintage finds.

Escondido
302 West Mission Avenue
(619) 696-9463

ROBERT MONDAVI WINE AND FOOD CENTER
Holds special private and public events. You can host a party here or attend one of their wine education or cooking classes. There are many programs available. This is a satellite Mondavi campus and the only one like it in the country. Look for cooking classes that focus on the foods of Europe, Asia, and South America. There's even talk of a summer concert series. This center is located in a business park (it may be hard to locate).

Costa Mesa (Orange County)
1570 Scenic Avenue
(714) 979-4510

SAN DIEGO WINE COMPANY
Offers discount wines from around the world.

Miramar
5282 Eastgate Mall
(858) 535-1400

SPIRITS OF ST. GERMAIN
Offers premium wines and gift baskets.

La Jolla
3251 Holiday Court
(858) 455-1414

THE SPIRIT SHOP
Offers wines and fine spirits.

La Jolla
2160 Avenida De La Playa
(858) 454-5252

TRADER JOE'S
Sells a large selection of everyday and quality wines at reduced prices.

Encinitas
115 North El Camino Real
(760) 634-2114

Hillcrest
1092 University Avenue
(619) 296-3122

La Jolla
8657 Villa La Jolla Drive
(858) 546-8629

La Mesa
5495 Grossmont Center Drive
(619) 466-0105

Pacific Beach
1211 Garnet Avenue
(619) 272-7235

Rancho Bernardo
11955 Carmel Mountain Road
(858) 673-0526

VILLAGE MARKET
Carries premium wines as well as Champagne and Sherry.

Rancho Santa Fe
16950 Via de Santa Fe
(858) 756-3726

VINTAGE WINES, LTD.
Well known for its Zinfandels, this shop has a wine bar and carries high-quality wines. Wine classes are also offered here.

Miramar
6904 Miramar Road
(858) 549-2112

WINE BANK
Sells wines at discount prices.

Gaslamp Quarter
363 Fifth Avenue, Suite 100
(619) 234-7487

THE WINE CONNECTION
Offers domestic and imported wines.

Del Mar
2650 Via De La Valle, C-130
(858) 350-9292

WINESELLAR & BRASSERIE
Large selection of premium and everyday wines.

Sorrento Mesa
9550 Waples Street
(858) 450-9557

WINE STREET
A North County shop with a nice selection (it also holds wine tastings).

Carlsbad
6986 El Camino Real
(760) 431-8455

You can also find a nice selection of wines at local grocery stores such as Vons, Ralphs, Whole Foods Market, and Price Club/Costco.

Wine Clubs

AMERICAN INSTITUTE OF WINE AND FOOD (AIWF)

This organization was founded by Julia Child and Robert Mondavi. Membership includes educational programs and events as well as newsletters and announcements of events. It is a national organization.

San Diego Chapter
2683 Via de la Valle
Del Mar, California 92014
(858) 847-9421
Website: www.aiwf.org

THE WINE BRATS

This organization hopes to get people, especially those under the age of 35, involved in wine. Membership includes quarterly meetings with no fee (except for an occasional small amount to cover wine costs).

(National Headquarters)
P.O. Box 5432
Santa Rosa, California 95402-5432
(877) 545-4699
Website: www.wine.brats.org

WINE FINDERS

A wine club offering wines at discounted prices. Two bottles are sent to your home each month.

1315-67th Street
Emeryville, California 94608-9843
(800) 845-8896
Website: www.winefinders.com

WINE OF THE MONTH CLUB

Membership is free and open to everyone. For information, write to the club.

Wine of the Month Club
116 West Lime Avenue
Monrovia, California 91016
(800) 949-WINE
Website: www.WineoftheMonthClub.com

Note: Most of the wineries listed in this book have wine clubs that will (for a fee) send you wine once a month. Check with the individual winery you are interested in.

SLOW FOOD USA

A movement begun by an Italian named Carlo Petrini, who was fed up with a McDonald's opening near the Spanish Steps in Rome, Italy. The movement focuses on promoting local consumption of fine, artisanal foods from local growers, including wineries.

434 Broadway, 6th Floor
New York, New York 10013
(212) 965-5640
Website: www.slowfoodusa.org

Websites

Wine.com
www.wine.com
Provides information about wine pertaining to tasting wine, pairing food with wine, types of wine, a glossary, and guides and resources. The site also sells wine by winery or growing region and by varietal.

The Wine Lovers Web Site
www.drinkwine.com
Includes information about wine and wineries, food, dining, references, and a "how to" section.

Wine Online
www.wine.net
Features a wide selection of premium wine brands with a search engine by name, varietal, price or region.

Wine Spectator Magazine
www.winespectator.com
Includes daily wine news, features, library, dining, travel, and more.

Suggested Trips

Below are tour ideas if you're having trouble deciding where to go to "partake of the grape."

BUDGET-CONSCIOUS TOUR

Drive to Bernardo Winery (where tasting wine is free). Then head to Escondido and go to Deer Park, Ferrara, and Orfila wineries. All of these wineries have no charge for tasting. Make your last stop Orfila winery and bring a picnic lunch to eat at one of their outdoor tables.

MOUNTAIN GETAWAY TOUR

Drive to Julian for the weekend and stay at one of the bed and breakfast inns mentioned in this book. Take a day to visit the Menghini, J. Jenkins, and Witch Creek tasting rooms. Call Menghini Winery; and ask when their art festival or grape stomp is (then visit during that weekend).

CELEBRATION TOUR

Rent a limo from one of the companies listed on page 75 and go to the Temecula Valley. Usually you have about five hours with the limo, including the drive up and back. Make sure to have your driver take you to Mount Palomar, Thornton, and Callaway wineries. You can take a tour at Callaway Winery. Then have lunch or dinner at Thornton Winery (call beforehand to find out when Thornton Winery is having their jazz series and go during that time), or have lunch at Carol's Restaurant.

MEXICAN TOUR

Take the Baja California Tour of Wineries and go to Château Camou, L.A. Cetto, and Casa Pedro Domecq wineries. Then have lunch at L.A. Cetto.

BEACH, WINE, AND SHOPPING TOUR

Drive to Carlsbad and visit Witch Creek Winery. Take some time to visit the antique shops nearby, then head to the Carlsbad Company Stores for more shopping. Afterward go to Bellefleur Restaurant for lunch or dinner and to sample wines.

Glossary

Acidity
Term used to describe the sharpness or tartness of a wine. Acids are found in all grapes and occur in wine naturally. You will sense this taste after you've swallowed the wine. Your mouth will be dry and you will salivate.

Aeration
The act of exposing wine to oxygen. This process can soften a wine. Some people put wine in carafes to aerate it.

Aging
Term that describes the process of storing wine over time to allow it to adopt a softer, more complex taste. Wines are usually aged in a barrel or bottle and sometimes in both.

Appellation
Can be the name of a vineyard, county, or district. It defines where the grapes are grown. If a California wine label states an appellation, it must consist of at least 85 percent of wine from that area.

Aroma
Term used to describe the overall smell of wine.

Astringency
Caused by tannin in wine from seeds and skins of grapes. Creates a puckery feel in the mouth.

Balance
This term includes the flavor and texture of wine, including the sweetness, acidity, tannin, and alcohol that come together to create a wholeness.

Botrytis Cinerea
A type of mold that shrivels grapes, leaving their flavor stronger and their sugar content higher.

Body
Term used to describe how heavy the wine feels in the mouth. The more alcohol a wine has, the more body it seems to have.

Bouquet
The wine's smell, which becomes stronger as the wine ages.

Brut
Describes an especially dry sparkling wine.

Carbonic Maceration
A process where whole grapes and their stems are fermented together in a closed container. The grapes are then pressed to extract the wine. The wine produced tends to be light and fruity.

Claret
A British term describing a red wine from Bordeaux that is aged for years in barrels.

Clarification
Process of removing sediment from fermented wine.

Clarity
How clear the wine looks in the glass.

Cortese
A white wine that can be described as rich and dry. It consists of different types of grapes.

Decant
To get clear wine, wine is poured from the bottle into a container called a decanter so that the sediment stays in the bottle.

Earthy

When a wine is described as "earthy," its scent or taste is of things that are found in the earth (this term describes both good and bad qualities).

Fermentation

A step in the winemaking process. There are two types of fermentation processes. One is alcoholic fermentation (sugars turn into alcohol) and the other is malolactic fermentation (malic acid turns into lactic acid).

Finish

The final feeling or taste after wine is swallowed. It is the lasting impression after wine has been in the mouth. When the finish is agreeable, it leaves the mouth wanting more.

Generic

These wines tend to be less expensive than varietal wines and are a combination of grape varieties.

Grassy

A word used to describe a wine that has tastes or aromas of grass, hay, or a hint of vegetable. The term has both good and bad connotations, depending on the opinion of the taster.

Heat Summation

Term used in California to describe the best place to grow wine grapes determined by an area's average daily temperature from April to October. Once the average temperature is determined, the areas are designated from Region I for the coolest areas through Region V for the warmest ones.

Jammy

A term used to describe the taste of wine when it has a heavy, jam-like flavor.

Late Harvest

Wines produced from grapes that have been picked after the regular harvest season. This process makes the wines sweeter. Dessert wines are usually made from late harvest grapes.

Lees
Residue of different ingredients, like yeast and grape parts, remaining in barrels after the fermentation process.

Legs
A pattern obtained by swirling a glass of wine. The wine lingers on the glass, creating a leg-like pattern on the sides. People sometimes mistake this process as an indication of a wine's quality, but actually it's a measure of the alcohol content.

Length
A portion of the number of taste buds along the tongue that the wine reaches and the total time the aroma and taste last after drinking the wine.

Must
The combination of grape juice, pulp, and skin obtained through crushing.

Non-vintage
Wines that do not have a vintage year on the label and are often blends of grapes from various years.

Nose
The combination of grape aroma and bouquet of wine.

Reserve
This name is sometimes given to a bottle of varietal wine that is more expensive than the regular bottles with the same varietal name. There is no legal standard for this name, so the meaning can vary from one winery to the next. Usually these wines have more flavor and have been aged longer than regular wines.

Residual Sugar
The type of sugar that stays after the wine ferments.

Sommelier
A person who is in charge of wines.

Sur Lie
A French saying that translates as "on the lees." This is an aging procedure where wines stay in contact with the dead yeast cells after fermentation.

Sweetness
This term is used to describe what the tongue experiences when tasting wine. Wines that have a sugary taste are given this term.

Tannin
In the skins, seeds, and stem of grapes, an antioxidant that slows the aging process of wine. Red wines have more tannin than white wines because they are fermented with their skins. Tannins act like a preservative and are the reason why red wines last (they are a crucial ingredient in aging wine). Tannin creates a "mouth puckery" reaction when tasted and leaves the mouth feeling dry.

Varietal
Wines made from one grape. For example, when a wine is labeled "Chardonnay," it must consist of 75 percent of that grape variety.

Vintage
Term to describe the harvesting year of the grape. When there is a vintage date on a bottle of wine, at least 95 percent of the grapes must be from that year.

Viscosity
Term used to describe wine's weight. Sometimes wine is described as watery, medium weight, heavy, or oily. This is the viscosity.

Viticultural Area/American Viticultural Area (AVA)
A type of appellation where winegrowers in certain areas will ask the government to grant them the right to put that area's name on their wine labels. If the right is granted, 85 percent of the wine in those bottles must be from that area.

Yeasty
Term used to describe the smell of yeast that may be likened to the smell of baking bread.

For Further Reading/Sources

Adams, Leon D. *The Commonsense Book of Wine*, New York: McGraw-Hill, 1986.

Austerman, John. *Baja California*, Los Angeles: Automobile Club of Southern California, 1991.

Barrow, Clare. *Julian,* San Diego's North County Magazine, Fall 1997.

Bernstein, Cal. *Wine! The Complete CD-ROM Guide*, March 1997.

Bespaloffs, Alexis. *Complete Guide to Wine*, New York: Penguin Books, 1994.

De Lude, Michelle. *California Winery Tours*, Los Angeles: Travel Publications Department, Automobile Club of Southern California, 1993.

Elwood, Ann. *Wineries, San Diego County and Temecula Valley*, Los Angeles: Chalk Press, 1999.

Ewing-Mulligan, Mary. *Entertaining–Wine Tasting 101*. Martha Stewart Living, May 1996.

Gaiter, Dorothy J. and John Brecher. "Giving American Rosés a Second Chance," *Wall Street Journal*, July 21, 1999.

Geiser, Angela. "Gioveto, Cortese & Viognier–Temecula
Wineries Shift Focus to Mediterranean Wines," *The
Daily Californian*, April 28, 1996.

Gleeson, Bill. *Backroad Wineries of Southern California, a
Scenic Tour of California Country Wineries*,
San Francisco: Chronicle Books, 1994.

Goldberg, Howard. "The Best White Wine of All?" *Saveur
Magazine*, May/June 1996.

Green, Richard. "Wine Drinkers Who Bother to Look at the
Cork May Find Plastic," *San Diego Union-Tribune*,
October 5, 1997.

Johnson, Hugh. *The World Atlas of Wine—The Wine Book of
The Century*, New York: Simon and Schuster, 1985.

Kornblum, Annette. "Should You Drink to Your Health?" *Better
Homes and Gardens*, October 1997.

MacNeil, Karen. "The Wine Guide." *Sunset Magazine* (every
issue).

MacNeil, Karen. "Wine Tasting Porch Pics." *Cooking Light*,
April 1999.

McCarthy, Ed. *Wine For Dummies*, Foster City, California: IDG
Books Worldwide, 1995.

Marsano, Bill. "The Grace of a Civilized Table." *Weight
Watchers Magazine*, May–June 1997.

Martin, Leslie. "The Puzzling Petite Sirah." *Country Living*,
October 1997.

Parker, Robert. "California Bargains–Bottles from Top Wineries
for $10 and Under." *Food & Wine Magazine*, May
1996.

Seff, Marsha Kay. "Julian, San Diego's Big Apple,"
San Diego Union-Tribune, October 20, 1996.

South Coast Wine Magazine

Staggs, Bill. "Why Wine is Really Better: New Research
     Shows the Fruit of the Vine is Rich in Compounds that
     Boost Alcohol's Benefits and May Dampen its Risks,"
     Health Magazine, January–February 1996.

Sunset Guide to California's Wine Country, Menlo Park,
     California: Lane Books, 1982.

Tarbell, Nick. "Grape Expectations–Recipe For a Wine Tasting,"
     Arizona Foothills, April 1999.

Thompson, Bob and Hugh Johnson. *The California Wine Book*, 1976.

Wheelock, Walt and Gulick, Howard. *Baja California
     Guidebook–a Descriptive Traveler's Guide*, Glendale,
     California: Arthur H. Clark Co. 1980.

Whitley, Robert. "Crystal Persuasion Not Just Any Glass,"
     San Diego Union-Tribune, May 29, 1997.

INDEX

Tasting Notes

Name of Wine

Winery

Vintage

Date of Tasting

Price

Color

This is where you record the **Clarity** (How defined is the wine?),
Depth (How mild or deep is it?), **Color** (If the wine is white, does it
look yellow or brown? If the wine is red, does it have hints of purple
or brown?), and **Viscosity** (Is the wine mild, average weight, weighty,
or slick?)

Smell

Here's where you record the **Appearance** (Is the wine indefinite,
distinct, noteworthy?), **Aroma** (Positive or negative?), and **Bouquet**
(Is there one? Is it agreeable, involved, or strong?)

Taste

List here the **Sweetness** (Sweet or dry?), **Tannin** (Does it have it?),
Acidity, **Body**, **Length**, and **Balance**.

Tasting Notes

Name of Wine	Winery

Vintage	Date of Tasting	Price

Color

This is where you record the **Clarity** (How defined is the wine?), **Depth** (How mild or deep is it?), **Color** (If the wine is white, does it look yellow or brown? If the wine is red, does it have hints of purple or brown?), and **Viscosity** (Is the wine mild, average weight, weighty, or slick?)

Smell

Here's where you record the **Appearance** (Is the wine indefinite, distinct, noteworthy?), **Aroma** (Positive or negative?), and **Bouquet** (Is there one? Is it agreeable, involved, or strong?)

Taste

List here the **Sweetness** (Sweet or dry?), **Tannin** (Does it have it?), **Acidity**, **Body**, **Length**, and **Balance**.

Tasting Notes

Name of Wine	Winery

Vintage	Date of Tasting	Price

Color

This is where you record the **Clarity** (How defined is the wine?), **Depth** (How mild or deep is it?), **Color** (If the wine is white, does it look yellow or brown? If the wine is red, does it have hints of purple or brown?), and **Viscosity** (Is the wine mild, average weight, weighty, or slick?)

Smell

Here's where you record the **Appearance** (Is the wine indefinite, distinct, noteworthy?), **Aroma** (Positive or negative?), and **Bouquet** (Is there one? Is it agreeable, involved, or strong?)

Taste

List here the **Sweetness** (Sweet or dry?), **Tannin** (Does it have it?), **Acidity**, **Body**, **Length**, and **Balance**.

Tasting Notes

Name of Wine	Winery

Vintage	Date of Tasting	Price

Color

This is where you record the **Clarity** (How defined is the wine?), **Depth** (How mild or deep is it?), **Color** (If the wine is white, does it look yellow or brown? If the wine is red, does it have hints of purple or brown?), and **Viscosity** (Is the wine mild, average weight, weighty, or slick?)

Smell

Here's where you record the **Appearance** (Is the wine indefinite, distinct, noteworthy?), **Aroma** (Positive or negative?), and **Bouquet** (Is there one? Is it agreeable, involved, or strong?)

Taste

List here the **Sweetness** (Sweet or dry?), **Tannin** (Does it have it?), **Acidity**, **Body**, **Length**, and **Balance**.

Tasting Notes

Name of Wine

Winery

Vintage

Date of Tasting

Price

Color

This is where you record the **Clarity** (How defined is the wine?), **Depth** (How mild or deep is it?), **Color** (If the wine is white, does it look yellow or brown? If the wine is red, does it have hints of purple or brown?), and **Viscosity** (Is the wine mild, average weight, weighty, or slick?)

Smell

Here's where you record the **Appearance** (Is the wine indefinite, distinct, noteworthy?), **Aroma** (Positive or negative?), and **Bouquet** (Is there one? Is it agreeable, involved, or strong?)

Taste

List here the **Sweetness** (Sweet or dry?), **Tannin** (Does it have it?), **Acidity**, **Body**, **Length**, and **Balance**.

Tasting Notes

Name of Wine

Winery

Vintage

Date of Tasting

Price

Color

This is where you record the **Clarity** (How defined is the wine?), **Depth** (How mild or deep is it?), **Color** (If the wine is white, does it look yellow or brown? If the wine is red, does it have hints of purple or brown?), and **Viscosity** (Is the wine mild, average weight, weighty, or slick?)

Smell

Here's where you record the **Appearance** (Is the wine indefinite, distinct, noteworthy?), **Aroma** (Positive or negative?), and **Bouquet** (Is there one? Is it agreeable, involved, or strong?)

Taste

List here the **Sweetness** (Sweet or dry?), **Tannin** (Does it have it?), **Acidity**, **Body**, **Length**, and **Balance**.

Tasting Notes

Name of Wine	Winery

Vintage	Date of Tasting	Price

Color

This is where you record the **Clarity** (How defined is the wine?), **Depth** (How mild or deep is it?), **Color** (If the wine is white, does it look yellow or brown? If the wine is red, does it have hints of purple or brown?), and **Viscosity** (Is the wine mild, average weight, weighty, or slick?)

Smell

Here's where you record the **Appearance** (Is the wine indefinite, distinct, noteworthy?), **Aroma** (Positive or negative?), and **Bouquet** (Is there one? Is it agreeable, involved, or strong?)

Taste

List here the **Sweetness** (Sweet or dry?), **Tannin** (Does it have it?), **Acidity**, **Body**, **Length**, and **Balance**.

Tasting Notes

Name of Wine

Winery

Vintage

Date of Tasting

Price

Color

This is where you record the **Clarity** (How defined is the wine?), **Depth** (How mild or deep is it?), **Color** (If the wine is white, does it look yellow or brown? If the wine is red, does it have hints of purple or brown?), and **Viscosity** (Is the wine mild, average weight, weighty, or slick?)

Smell

Here's where you record the **Appearance** (Is the wine indefinite, distinct, noteworthy?), **Aroma** (Positive or negative?), and **Bouquet** (Is there one? Is it agreeable, involved, or strong?)

Taste

List here the **Sweetness** (Sweet or dry?), **Tannin** (Does it have it?), **Acidity**, **Body**, **Length**, and **Balance**.

Tasting Notes

Name of Wine	Winery

Vintage	Date of Tasting	Price

Color

This is where you record the **Clarity** (How defined is the wine?), **Depth** (How mild or deep is it?), **Color** (If the wine is white, does it look yellow or brown? If the wine is red, does it have hints of purple or brown?), and **Viscosity** (Is the wine mild, average weight, weighty, or slick?)

Smell

Here's where you record the **Appearance** (Is the wine indefinite, distinct, noteworthy?), **Aroma** (Positive or negative?), and **Bouquet** (Is there one? Is it agreeable, involved, or strong?)

Taste

List here the **Sweetness** (Sweet or dry?), **Tannin** (Does it have it?), **Acidity**, **Body**, **Length**, and **Balance**.

Tasting Notes

Name of Wine	Winery

Vintage	Date of Tasting	Price

Color

This is where you record the **Clarity** (How defined is the wine?), **Depth** (How mild or deep is it?), **Color** (If the wine is white, does it look yellow or brown? If the wine is red, does it have hints of purple or brown?), and **Viscosity** (Is the wine mild, average weight, weighty, or slick?)

Smell

Here's where you record the **Appearance** (Is the wine indefinite, distinct, noteworthy?), **Aroma** (Positive or negative?), and **Bouquet** (Is there one? Is it agreeable, involved, or strong?)

Taste

List here the **Sweetness** (Sweet or dry?), **Tannin** (Does it have it?), **Acidity**, **Body**, **Length**, and **Balance**.

Tasting Notes

Name of Wine	Winery

Vintage	Date of Tasting	Price

Color

This is where you record the **Clarity** (How defined is the wine?), **Depth** (How mild or deep is it?), **Color** (If the wine is white, does it look yellow or brown? If the wine is red, does it have hints of purple or brown?), and **Viscosity** (Is the wine mild, average weight, weighty, or slick?)

Smell

Here's where you record the **Appearance** (Is the wine indefinite, distinct, noteworthy?), **Aroma** (Positive or negative?), and **Bouquet** (Is there one? Is it agreeable, involved, or strong?)

Taste

List here the **Sweetness** (Sweet or dry?), **Tannin** (Does it have it?), **Acidity**, **Body**, **Length**, and **Balance**.

Tasting Notes

Name of Wine

Winery

Vintage

Date of Tasting

Price

Color

This is where you record the **Clarity** (How defined is the wine?), **Depth** (How mild or deep is it?), **Color** (If the wine is white, does it look yellow or brown? If the wine is red, does it have hints of purple or brown?), and **Viscosity** (Is the wine mild, average weight, weighty, or slick?)

Smell

Here's where you record the **Appearance** (Is the wine indefinite, distinct, noteworthy?), **Aroma** (Positive or negative?), and **Bouquet** (Is there one? Is it agreeable, involved, or strong?)

Taste

List here the **Sweetness** (Sweet or dry?), **Tannin** (Does it have it?), **Acidity**, **Body**, **Length**, and **Balance**.

Order Form

Mail to:

Popcorn Press & Media, Janene Roberts, P.O. Box 900039
San Diego, CA 92190-0039

Please send _____ copies of *Wine Tasting in San Diego & Beyond* to:

Name:_____

Address:_____

City:_____ State:_____ ZIP:_____-_____

Telephone: (____) _____

Cost: # of books____@$15.95 $_____
$15.95 each

Sales Tax: Sales tax $_____
A 7.75% sales tax applies only if book is being sent to a California
address.

Shipping ($2.25 per book):   Shipping & Handling $_____
(Please allow three to four weeks for delivery)
Air mail rate is $4 to arrive within one week.

Please enclose payment.   **TOTAL ENCLOSED** $_____

Order Today!